TOM STOPPARD was catapulted into the front ranks of modern playwrights overnight when *Rosencrantz and Guildenstern Are Dead* opened in London in 1967. Its subsequent run in New York brought it the same enthusiastic acclaim, and the play has since been performed numerous times in the major theatrical centers of the world. It has won top honors for a play and playwright in a poll of London Theater critics, and in its printed form it was chosen one of the "Notable Books of 1967" by the American Library Association.

"Stoppard is the master comedian of ideas in the English language," Jack Kroll said about him in *Newsweek*. Each of his stage works has confirmed this view. Theatergoers have been able to admire his wit and thrill to his command of the English language in *Jumpers, The Real Inspector Hound, Travesties, Enter A Free Man, After Magritte,* and *Dirty Linen* and *New-Found-Land*. He is also the author of the novel *Lord Malquist and Mr. Moon*.

Rosencrantz & Guildenstern Are Dead

WORKS BY TOM STOPPARD
PUBLISHED BY GROVE PRESS

Every Good Boy Deserves Favor and *Professional Foul*

Jumpers

The Real Inspector Hound and Other Plays

Rosencrantz and Guildenstern Are Dead

Travesties

The Invention of Love

Rosencrantz
&
Guildenstern
Are
Dead

---

by Tom Stoppard

Consulting editor: Henry Popkin

GROVE PRESS
NEW YORK

The first performance of *Rosencrantz and Guildenstern Are Dead* was given in a slightly shortened form on August 24, 1966 at Cranston Street Hall, Edinburgh, by the Oxford Theatre Group as part of the "fringe" of the Edinburgh Festival. The cast was as follows:

ROSENCRANTZ	David Marks
GUILDENSTERN	Clive Cable
THE PLAYER	Jules Roach
TRAGEDIANS	Ron Forfar, Nic Renton, Howard Daubney
HAMLET	John Dodgson
OPHELIA	Janet Watts
CLAUDIUS	Nick Elliot
GERTRUDE	Frances Morrow
POLONIUS	Walter Merricks

Directed by Brian Daubney

The first professional production was given on April 11, 1967 at the Old Vic Theatre, London, by the National Theatre Company. The cast was as follows:

ROSENCRANTZ	John Stride
GUILDENSTERN	Edward Petherbridge
THE PLAYER	Graham Crowden
ALFRED	Alan Adams
TRAGEDIANS	Oliver Cotton, Neil Fitzpatrick, Luke Hardy, Roger Kemp
HAMLET	John McEnery
OPHELIA	Caroline John
CLAUDIUS	Kenneth Mackintosh
GERTRUDE	Mary Griffiths
POLONIUS	Peter Cellier
HORATIO	David Hargreaves
FORTINBRAS	David Bailie
AMBASSADOR	David Ryall
1ST SOLDIER	Christopher Timothy
2ND SOLDIER	Denis de Marne

COURT AND ATTENDANTS
Petronella Barker, Margo Cunningham, Kay Gallie, David Belcher, Reginald Green, William Hobbs, Lennard Pearce, Ron Pember, Frederick Pyne

Directed by Derek Goldby
Designed by Desmond Heeley

The New York première of *Rosencrantz and Guildenstern Are Dead* was given on October 16, 1967 at the Alvin Theatre. The cast was as follows:

ROSENCRANTZ	Brian Murray
GUILDENSTERN	John Wood
THE PLAYER	Paul Hecht
ALFRED	Douglas Norwick
TRAGEDIANS	Roger Kemp, Dino Laudicina, B. J. DeSimone, Roy Lozano
HAMLET	Noel Craig
OPHELIA	Pat McAneny
CLAUDIUS	Roger Hamilton
GERTRUDE	Anne Meacham
POLONIUS	Ralph Drischell
SOLDIER	Alexander Courtney
HORATIO	Michael Holmes

COURTIERS, AMBASSADORS, SOLDIERS, AND ATTENDANTS
Walter Beery, Stephen Bernstein, Gaetano Bon Giovanni, Margaret Braidwood, Esther Buffler, Alexander Courtney, Elizabeth Eis, Elizabeth Franz, William Grannell, John Handy, Mary Hara, Carl Jacobs, Ed Marshall, Ted Pezzulo, Jonathan Reynolds

MUSICIANS
Bruce Levine, Arthur Lora, Bernie Karl, Jack Knitzer

Directed by Derek Goldby

Designed by Desmond Heeley

Rosencrantz & Guildenstern Are Dead

ACT ONE

Two ELIZABETHANS *passing the time in a place without any visible character.*

They are well dressed—hats, cloaks, sticks and all.

Each of them has a large leather money bag.

GUILDENSTERN'*s bag is nearly empty.*

ROSENCRANTZ'*s bag is nearly full.*

The reason being: they are betting on the toss of a coin, in the following manner: GUILDENSTERN *(hereafter "*GUIL*") takes a coin out of his bag, spins it, letting it fall.* ROSENCRANTZ *(hereafter "*ROS*") studies it, announces it as "heads" (as it happens) and puts it into his own bag. Then they repeat the process. They have apparently been doing this for some time.*

The run of "heads" is impossible, yet ROS *betrays no surprise at all—he feels none. However, he is nice enough to feel a little embarrassed at taking so much money off his friend. Let that be his character note.*

GUIL *is well alive to the oddity of it. He is not worried about the money, but he is worried by the implications; aware but not going to panic about it—his character note.*

GUIL *sits.* ROS *stands (he does the moving, retrieving coins).*
GUIL *spins.* ROS *studies coin.*

ROS: Heads.

> *He picks it up and puts it in his bag. The process is repeated.*

Heads.

11

Again.

Heads.

Again.

Heads.

Again.

Heads.

GUIL (*flipping a coin*): There is an art to the building up of suspense.

ROS: Heads.

GUIL (*flipping another*): Though it can be done by luck alone.

ROS: Heads.

GUIL: If that's the word I'm after.

ROS (*raises his head at* GUIL): Seventy-six—love.

> GUIL *gets up but has nowhere to go. He spins another coin over his shoulder without looking at it, his attention being directed at his environment or lack of it.*

Heads.

GUIL: A weaker man might be moved to re-examine his faith, if in nothing else at least in the law of probability. (*He slips a coin over his shoulder as he goes to look upstage.*)

ROS: Heads.

> GUIL, *examining the confines of the stage, flips over two more coins as he does so, one by one of course.* ROS *announces each of them as "heads."*

GUIL (*musing*): The law of probability, it has been oddly asserted, is something to do with the proposition that if six monkeys (*he has surprised himself*) . . . if six monkeys were . . .

ROS: Game?

GUIL: Were they?

ROS: Are you?

GUIL (*understanding*): Game. (*Flips a coin.*) The law of averages, if I have got this right, means that if six monkeys were thrown up in the air for long enough they would land on their tails about as often as they would land on their——

ROS: Heads. (*He picks up the coin.*)

GUIL: Which even at first glance does not strike one as a particularly rewarding speculation, in either sense, even without the monkeys. I mean you wouldn't *bet* on it. I mean *I* would, but *you* wouldn't.... (*As he flips a coin.*)

ROS: Heads.

GUIL: Would you? (*Flips a coin.*)

ROS: Heads.

Repeat.

Heads. (*He looks up at* GUIL—*embarrassed laugh.*) Getting a bit of a bore, isn't it?

GUIL (*coldly*): A bore?

ROS: Well ...

GUIL: What about the suspense?

ROS (innocently): What suspense?

Small pause.

GUIL: It must be the law of diminishing returns. ... I feel the spell about to be broken. (*Energizing himself somewhat. He takes out a coin, spins it high, catches it, turns it over on to the back of his other hand, studies the coin—and tosses it to* ROS. *His energy deflates and he sits.*)

Well, it was an even chance ... if my calculations are correct.

13

ROS: Eighty-five in a row—beaten the record!

GUIL: Don't be absurd.

ROS: Easily!

GUIL (*angry*): Is that *it*, then? Is that all?

ROS: What?

GUIL: A new record? Is that as far as you are prepared to go?

ROS: Well . . .

GUIL: No questions? Not even a pause?

ROS: You spun them yourself.

GUIL: Not a flicker of doubt?

ROS (*aggrieved, aggressive*): Well, I won—didn't I?

GUIL (*approaches him—quieter*): And if you'd lost? If they'd come down against you, eighty-five times, one after another, just like that?

ROS (*dumbly*): Eighty-five in a row? *Tails?*

GUIL: Yes! What would you think?

ROS (*doubtfully*): Well . . . . (*Jocularly.*) Well, I'd have a good look at your coins for a start!

GUIL (*retiring*): I'm relieved. At least we can still count on self-interest as a predictable factor. . . . I suppose it's the last to go. Your capacity for trust made me wonder if perhaps . . . you, alone . . . (*He turns on him suddenly, reaches out a hand.*) Touch.

ROS *clasps his hand.* GUIL *pulls him up to him.*

GUIL (*more intensely*): We have been spinning coins together since—— (*He releases him almost as violently.*) This is not the first time we have spun coins!

14

ROS: Oh no—we've been spinning coins for as long as I remember.

GUIL: How long is that?

ROS: I forget. Mind you—eighty-five times!

GUIL: Yes?

ROS: It'll take some beating, I imagine.

GUIL: Is *that* what you imagine? Is that it? No *fear?*

ROS: Fear?

GUIL (*in fury—flings a coin on the ground*): *Fear!* The crack that might flood your brain with light!

ROS: Heads. . . . (*He puts it in his bag.*)

> GUIL *sits despondently. He takes a coin, spins it, lets it fall between his feet. He looks at it, picks it up, throws it to* ROS, *who puts it in his bag.*
>
> GUIL *takes another coin, spins it, catches it, turns it over on to his other hand, looks at it, and throws it to* ROS, *who puts it in his bag.*
>
> GUIL *takes a third coin, spins it, catches it in his right hand, turns it over onto his left wrist, lobs it in the air, catches it with his left hand, raises his left leg, throws the coin up under it, catches it and turns it over on the top of his head, where it sits.* ROS *comes, looks at it, puts it in his bag.*

ROS: I'm afraid——

GUIL: So am I.

ROS: I'm afraid it isn't your day.

GUIL: I'm afraid it is.

> *Small pause.*

ROS: Eighty-nine.

GUIL: It must be indicative of something, besides the redistribution of wealth. (*He muses.*) List of possible explanations. One: I'm willing it. Inside where nothing shows, I am the essence of a man spinning double-headed coins, and betting against himself in private atonement for an unremembered past. (*He spins a coin at* ROS.)

ROS: Heads.

GUIL: Two: time has stopped dead, and the single experience of one coin being spun once has been repeated ninety times. . . . (*He flips a coin, looks at it, tosses it to* ROS.) On the whole, doubtful. Three: divine intervention, that is to say, a good turn from above concerning him, cf. children of Israel, or retribution from above concerning me, cf. Lot's wife. Four: a spectacular vindication of the principle that each individual coin spun individually (*he spins one*) is as likely to come down heads as tails and therefore should cause no surprise each individual time it does. (*It does. He tosses it to* ROS.)

ROS: I've never known anything like it!

GUIL: And a syllogism: One, he has never known anything like it. Two, he has never known anything to write home about. Three, it is nothing to write home about. . . . Home . . . What's the first thing you remember?

ROS: Oh, let's see. . . . The first thing that comes into my head, you mean?

GUIL: No—the first thing you remember.

ROS: Ah. (*Pause.*) No, it's no good, it's gone. It was a long time ago.

GUIL (*patient but edged*): You don't get my meaning. What is the first thing after all the things you've forgotten?

ROS: Oh I see. (*Pause.*) I've forgotten the question.

GUIL *leaps up and paces.*

16

GUIL: Are you happy?

ROS: What?

GUIL: Content? At ease?

ROS: I suppose so.

GUIL: What are you going to do now?

ROS: I don't know. What do you want to do?

GUIL: I have no desires. None. (*He stops pacing dead.*) There was a messenger . . . that's right. We were sent for. (*He wheels at* ROS *and raps out:*) Syllogism the second: One, probability is a factor which operates within natural forces. Two, probability is not operating as a factor. Three, we are now within un-, sub- or supernatural forces. Discuss. (ROS *is suitably startled. Acidly.*) Not too heatedly.

ROS: I'm sorry I—What's the matter with you?

GUIL: The scientific approach to the examination of phenomena is a defence against the pure emotion of fear. Keep tight hold and continue while there's time. Now— counter to the previous syllogism: tricky one, follow me carefully, it may prove a comfor. If we postulate, and we just have, that within un-, sub- or supernatural forces *the probability is* that the law of probability will not operate as a factor, then we must accept that the probability of the *first* part will not operate as a factor, in which case the law of probability *will* operate as a factor within un-, sub- or supernatural forces. And since it obviously hasn't been doing so, we can take it that we are not held within un-, sub- or supernatural forces after all; in all probability, that is. Which is a great relief to me personally. (*Small pause.*) Which is all very well, except that——(*He continues with tight hysteria, under control.*) We have been spinning coins together since I don't know when, and in all that time (if it *is* all that time) I don't suppose either of us was more than

17

a couple of gold pieces up or down. I hope that doesn't
sound surprising because its very unsurprisingness is
something I am trying to keep hold of. The equanimity of
your average tosser of coins depends upon a law, or
rather a tendency, or let us say a probability, or at
any rate a mathematically calculable chance, which ensures
that he will not upset himself by losing too much nor upset
his opponent by winning too often. This made for a kind of
harmony and a kind of confidence. It related the fortuitous
and the ordained into a reassuring union which we
recognized as nature. The sun came up about as often as it
went down, in the long run, and a coin showed heads about
as often as it showed tails. Then a messenger arrived. We
had been sent for. Nothing else happened. Ninety-two coins
spun consecutively have come down heads ninety-two
consecutive times . . . and for the last three minutes on the
wind of a windless day I have heard the sound of drums
and flute. . . .

ROS (*cutting his fingernails*): Another curious scientific
  phenomenon is the fact that the fingernails grow after
  death, as does the beard.

GUIL: What?

ROS (*loud*): Beard!

GUIL: But you're not dead.

ROS (*irritated*): I didn't say they *started* to grow after death!
  (*Pause, calmer.*) The fingernails also grow before birth,
  though *not* the beard.

GUIL: *What?*

ROS (*shouts*): Beard! What's the matter with you? (*Reflectively.*)
  The toenails, on the other hand, never grow at all.

GUIL (*bemused*): The toenails never grow at all?

ROS: Do they? It's a funny thing—I cut my fingernails all the time, and every time I think to cut them, they need cutting. Now, for instance. And yet, I never, to the best of my knowledge, cut my toenails. They ought to be curled under my feet by now, but it doesn't happen. I never think about them. Perhaps I cut them absent-mindedly, when I'm thinking of something else.

GUIL (*tensed up by this rambling*): Do you remember the first thing that happened today?

ROS (*promptly*): I woke up, I suppose. (*Triggered.*) Oh—I've got it now—that man, a foreigner, he woke us up——

GUIL: A messenger. (*He relaxes, sits.*)

ROS: That's it—pale sky before dawn, a man standing on his saddle to bang on the shutters—shouts—What's all the row about?! Clear off!—But then he called our names. You remember that—this man woke us up.

GUIL: Yes.

ROS: We were sent for.

GUIL: Yes.

ROS: That's why we're here. (*He looks round, seems doubtful, then the explanation.*) Travelling.

GUIL: Yes.

ROS (*dramatically*): It was urgent—a matter of extreme urgency, a royal summons, his very words: official business and no questions asked—lights in the stable-yard, saddle up and off headlong and hotfoot across the land, our guides outstripped in breakneck pursuit of our duty! Fearful lest we come too late!!

Small pause.

GUIL: Too late for what?

ROS: How do I know? We haven't got there yet.

GUIL: Then what are we doing here, I ask myself.

ROS: You might well ask.

GUIL: We better get on.

ROS: You might well think.

GUIL: We better get on.

ROS (*actively*): Right! (*Pause.*) On where?

GUIL: Forward.

ROS (*forward to footlights*): Ah. (*Hesitates.*) Which way do we——(*He turns round.*) Which way did we——?

GUIL: Practically starting from scratch. . . . An awakening, a man standing on his saddle to bang on the shutters, our names shouted in a certain dawn, a message, a summons . . . A new record for heads and tails. We have not been . . . picked out . . . simply to be abandoned . . . set loose to find our own way. . . . We are entitled to some direction. . . . I would have thought.

ROS (*alert, listening*): I say——! I say——

GUIL: Yes?

ROS: I can hear—I thought I heard—music.

GUIL *raises himself.*

GUIL: Yes?

ROS: Like a band. (*He looks around, laughs embarrassedly, expiating himself.*) It sounded like—a band. Drums.

GUIL: Yes.

ROS (*relaxes*): It couldn't have been real.

GUIL: "The colours red, blue and green are real. The colour yellow is a mystical experience shared by everybody"—demolish.

20

ROS (*at edge of stage*): It must have been thunder. Like drums . . .

By the end of the next speech, the band is faintly audible.

GUIL: A man breaking his journey between one place and
   another at a third place of no name, character, population
   or significance, sees a unicorn cross his path and disappear.
   That in itself is startling, but there are precedents for
   mystical encounters of various kinds, or to be less extreme,
   a choice of persuasions to put it down to fancy; until—
   "My God," says a second man, "I must be dreaming, I
   thought I saw a unicorn." At which point, a dimension is
   added that makes the experience as alarming as it will ever
   be. A third witness, you understand, adds no further
   dimension but only spreads it thinner, and a fourth thinner
   still, and the more witnesses there are the thinner it gets and
   the more reasonable it becomes until it is as thin as reality,
   the name we give to the common experience. . . . "Look,
   look!" recites the crowd. "A horse with an arrow in its
   forehead! It must have been mistaken for a deer."

ROS (*eagerly*): I knew all along it was a band.

GUIL (*tiredly*): He knew all along it was a band.

ROS: Here they come!

GUIL (*at the last moment before they enter—wistfully*): I'm sorry
   it wasn't a unicorn. It would have been nice to have
   unicorns.

The TRAGEDIANS *are six in number, including a small* BOY
(ALFRED). *Two pull and push a cart piled with props and
belongings. There is also a* DRUMMER, *a* HORN-PLAYER *and a*
FLAUTIST. *The* SPOKESMAN *("the* PLAYER") *has no instrument.
He brings up the rear and is the first to notice them.*

PLAYER: Halt!

The group turns and halts.

(*Joyously.*) An audience!

21

ROS *and* GUIL *half rise.*

Don't move!

They sink back. He regards them fondly.

Perfect! A lucky thing we came along.

ROS: For us?

PLAYER: Let us hope so. But to meet two gentlemen on the road—we would not hope to meet them off it.

ROS: No?

PLAYER: Well met, in fact, and just in time.

ROS: Why's that?

PLAYER: Why, we grow rusty and you catch us at the very point of decadence—by this time tomorrow we might have forgotten everything we ever knew. That's a thought, isn't it? (*He laughs generously.*) We'd be back where we started —improvising.

ROS: Tumblers, are you?

PLAYER: We can give you a tumble if that's your taste, and times being what they are. . . . Otherwise, for a jingle of coin we can do you a selection of gory romances, full of fine cadence and corpses, pirated from the Italian; and it doesn't take much to make a jingle—even a single coin has music in it.

They all flourish and bow, raggedly.

Tragedians, at your command.

ROS *and* GUIL *have got to their feet.*

ROS: My name is Guildenstern, and this is Rosencrantz.

GUIL *confers briefly with him.*

(*Without embarrassment.*) I'm sorry—*his* name's Guildenstern, and *I'm* Rosencrantz.

22

PLAYER: A pleasure. We've played to bigger, of course, but quality counts for something. I recognized you at once——

ROS: And who are we?

PLAYER: —as fellow artists.

ROS: I thought we were gentlemen.

PLAYER: For some of us it is performance, for others, patronage. They are two sides of the same coin, or, let us say, being as there are so many of us, the same side of two coins. (*Bows again.*) Don't clap too loudly—it's a very old world.

ROS: What is your line?

PLAYER: Tragedy, sir. Deaths and disclosures, universal and particular, denouements both unexpected and inexorable, transvestite melodrama on all levels including the suggestive. We transport you into a world of intrigue and illusion . . . clowns, if you like, murderers—we can do you ghosts and battles, on the skirmish level, heroes, villains, tormented lovers—set pieces in the poetic vein; we can do you rapiers or rape or both, by all means, faithless wives and ravished virgins—*flagrante delicto* at a price, but that comes under realism for which there are special terms. Getting warm, am I?

ROS (*doubtfully*): Well, I don't know. . . .

PLAYER: It costs little to watch, and little more if you happen to get caught up in the action, if that's your taste and times being what they are.

ROS: What are they?

PLAYER: Indifferent.

ROS: Bad?

PLAYER: Wicked. Now what precisely is your pleasure? (*He turns to the* TRAGEDIANS.) Gentlemen, disport yourselves.

The TRAGEDIANS *shuffle into some kind of line.*

There! See anything you like?

ROS (*doubtful, innocent*): What do they do?

PLAYER: Let your imagination run riot. They are beyond
    surprise.

ROS: And how much?

PLAYER: To take part?

ROS: To watch.

PLAYER: Watch what?

ROS: A private performance.

PLAYER: How private?

ROS: Well, there are only two of us. Is that enough?

PLAYER: For an audience, disappointing. For voyeurs, about
    average. .

ROS: What's the difference?

PLAYER: Ten guilders.

ROS (*horrified*): Ten *guilders*!

PLAYER: I mean eight.

ROS: Together?

PLAYER: Each. I don't think you understand—

ROS: What are you *saying*?

PLAYER: What am I saying—seven.

ROS: Where have you *been*?

PLAYER: Roundabout. A nest of children carries the custom of
    the town. Juvenile companies, they are the fashion. But
    they cannot match our repertoire . . . we'll stoop to
    anything if that's your bent. . . .

He regards ROS *meaningfully but* ROS *returns the stare blankly.*

ROS: They'll grow up.

PLAYER (*giving up*): There's one born every minute. (*To* TRAGEDIANS:) On-ward!

The TRAGEDIANS *start to resume their burdens and their journey.* GUIL *stirs himself at last.*

GUIL: Where are you going?

PLAYER: Ha-alt!

They halt and turn.

Home, sir.

GUIL: Where from?

PLAYER: Home. We're travelling people. We take our chances where we find them.

GUIL: It was chance, then?

PLAYER: Chance?

GUIL: You found us.

PLAYER: Oh yes.

GUIL: You were looking?

PLAYER: Oh no.

GUIL: Chance, then.

PLAYER: Or fate.

GUIL: Yours or ours?

PLAYER: It could hardly be one without the other.

GUIL: Fate, then.

PLAYER: Oh yes. We have no control. Tonight we play to the court. Or the night after. Or to the tavern. Or not.

GUIL: Perhaps I can use my influence.

PLAYER: At the tavern?

GUIL: At the court. I would say I have some influence.

PLAYER: Would you say so?

GUIL: I have influence yet.

PLAYER: Yet what?

GUIL seizes the PLAYER violently.

GUIL: I have influence!

The PLAYER does not resist. GUIL loosens his hold.

(*More calmly.*) You said something—about getting caught up in the action——

PLAYER (*gaily freeing himself*): I did!—I did!—You're quicker than your friend. . . . (*Confidingly.*) Now for a handful of guilders I happen to have a private and uncut performance of *The Rape of the Sabine Women*—or rather woman, or rather Alfred——(*Over his shoulder.*) Get your skirt on, Alfred——

The BOY starts struggling into a female robe.

. . . and for eight you can participate.

GUIL backs, PLAYER follows.

. . . taking either part.

GUIL backs.

. . . or both for ten.

GUIL tries to turn away, PLAYER holds his sleeve.

. . . with encores——

GUIL smashes the PLAYER across the face. The PLAYER recoils. GUIL stands trembling.

26

(*Resigned and quiet*). Get your skirt off, Alfred. . . .

ALFRED *struggles out of his half-on robe.*

GUIL (*shaking with rage and fright*): It could have been—it didn't have to be *obscene*. . . . It could have been—a bird out of season, dropping bright-feathered on my shoulder. . . . It could have been a tongueless dwarf standing by the road to point the way. . . . I was *prepared*. But it's this, is it? No enigma, no dignity, nothing classical, portentous, only this —a comic pornographer and a rabble of prostitutes. . . .

PLAYER (*acknowledging the description with a sweep of his hat, bowing; sadly*): You should have caught us in better times. We were purists then. (*Straightens up.*) On-ward.

The PLAYERS *make to leave.*

ROS (*his voice has changed: he has caught on*): Excuse me!

PLAYER: Ha-alt!

They halt.

A-al-l-fred!

ALFRED *resumes the struggle. The* PLAYER *comes forward.*

ROS: You're not—ah—exclusively players, then?

PLAYER: We're inclusively players, sir.

ROS: So you give—exhibitions?

PLAYER: Performances, sir.

ROS: Yes, of course. There's more money in that, is there?

PLAYER: There's more trade, sir.

ROS: Times being what they are.

PLAYER: Yes.

ROS: Indifferent.

PLAYER: Completely.

ROS: You know I'd no idea——

PLAYER: No——

ROS: I mean, I've *heard* of—but I've never actually——

PLAYER: No.

ROS: I mean, what exactly do you *do*?

PLAYER: We keep to our usual stuff, more or less, only inside out. We do on stage the things that are supposed to happen off. Which is a kind of integrity, if you look on every exit being an entrance somewhere else.

ROS (*nervy, loud*): Well, I'm not really the type of man who— no, but don't hurry off—sit down and tell us about some of the things people ask you to do——

The PLAYER *turns away.*

PLAYER: On-ward!

ROS: Just a minute!

They turn and look at him without expression.

Well, all right—I wouldn't mind seeing—just an idea of the kind of—(*Bravely.*) What will you do for that? (*And tosses a single coin on the ground between them.*)

The PLAYER *spits at the coin, from where he stands.*

The TRAGEDIANS *demur, trying to get at the coin. He kicks and cuffs them back.*

On!

ALFRED *is still half in and out of his robe. The* PLAYER *cuffs him.*

(*To* ALFRED:) What are you playing at?

28

ROS *is shamed into fury.*

ROS: Filth! Disgusting—I'll report you to the authorities—*perverts*! I know your game all right, it's all filth!

The PLAYERS *are about to leave.* GUIL *has remained detached.*

GUIL (*casually*): Do you like a bet?

The TRAGEDIANS *turn and look interested. The* PLAYER *comes forward.*

PLAYER: What kind of bet did you have in mind?

GUIL *walks half the distance towards the* PLAYER, *stops with his foot over the coin.*

GUIL: Double or quits.

PLAYER: Well . . . heads.

GUIL *raises his foot. The* PLAYER *bends. The* TRAGEDIANS *crowd round. Relief and congratulations. The* PLAYER *picks up the coin.* GUIL *throws him a second coin.*

GUIL: Again?

Some of the TRAGEDIANS *are for it, others against.*

GUIL: Evens.

The PLAYER *nods and tosses the coin.*

GUIL: Heads.

It is. He picks it up.

Again.

GUIL *spins coin.*

PLAYER: Heads.

It is. PLAYER *picks up coin. He has two coins again. He spins one.*

GUIL: Heads.

> *It is.* GUIL *picks it up. Then tosses it immediately.*

PLAYER (*fractional hesitation*): Tails.

> *But it's heads.* GUIL *picks it up.* PLAYER *tosses down his last coin by way of paying up, and turns away.* GUIL *doesn't pick it up; he puts his foot on it.*

GUIL: Heads.

PLAYER: No!

> *Pause. The* TRAGEDIANS *are against this.*

> (*Apologetically.*) They don't like the odds.

GUIL (*lifts his foot, squats; picks up the coin still squatting; looks up*): You were right—heads. (*Spins it, slaps his hand on it, on the floor.*) Heads I win.

PLAYER: No.

GUIL (*uncovers coin*): Right again. (*Repeat.*) Heads I win.

PLAYER: No.

GUIL (*uncovers coin*): And right again. (*Repeat.*) Heads I win.

PLAYER: *No!*

> *He turns away, the* TRAGEDIANS *with him.* GUIL *stands up, comes close.*

GUIL: Would you believe it? (*Stands back, relaxes, smiles.*) Bet me the year of my birth doubled is an odd number.

PLAYER: *Your* birth——!

GUIL: If you don't trust me don't bet with me.

PLAYER: Would you trust *me*?

GUIL: *Bet* me then.

PLAYER: My birth?

GUIL: Odd numbers you win.

PLAYER: You're on——

The TRAGEDIANS *have come forward, wide awake.*

GUIL: Good. Year of your birth. Double it. Even numbers I win, odd numbers I lose.

Silence. An awful sigh as the TRAGEDIANS *realize that any number doubled is even. Then a terrible row as they object. Then a terrible silence.*

PLAYER: We have no money.

GUIL *turns to him.*

GUIL: Ah. Then what *have* you got?

The PLAYER *silently brings* ALFRED *forward.* GUIL *regards* ALFRED *sadly.*

Was it for this?

PLAYER: It's the best we've got.

GUIL (*looking up and around*): Then the times are bad indeed.

The PLAYER *starts to speak, protestation, but* GUIL *turns on him viciously.*

The very *air* stinks.

The PLAYER *moves back.* GUIL *moves down to the footlights and turns.*

Come here, Alfred.

ALFRED *moves down and stands, frightened and small.*

(*Gently.*) Do you lose often?

ALFRED: Yes, sir.

GUIL: Then what could you have left to lose?

ALFRED: Nothing, sir.

Pause. GUIL *regards him.*

GUIL: Do you like being . . . an actor?

ALFRED: No, sir.

GUIL *looks around, at the audience.*

GUIL: You and I, Alfred—we could create a dramatic precedent here.

And ALFRED, *who has been near tears, starts to sniffle.*

Come, come, Alfred, this is no way to fill the theatres of Europe.

The PLAYER *has moved down, to remonstrate with* ALFRED. GUIL *cuts him off again.*

(*Viciously.*) Do you know any good plays?

PLAYER: Plays?

ROS (*coming forward, faltering shyly*): Exhibitions. . . .

GUIL: I thought you said you were actors.

PLAYER (*dawning*): Oh. Oh well, we *are*. We are. But there hasn't been much call——

GUIL: You lost. Well then—one of the Greeks, perhaps? You're familiar with the tragedies of antiquity, are you? The great homicidal classics? Matri, patri, fratri, sorrori, uxori and it goes without saying——

ROS: Saucy——

GUIL: —Suicidal—hm? Maidens aspiring to godheads——

ROS: And vice versa——

GUIL: Your kind of thing, is it?

32

PLAYER: Well, no, I can't say it is, really. We're more of the blood, love and rhetoric school.

GUIL: Well, I'll leave the choice to you, if there is anything to choose between them.

PLAYER: They're hardly divisible, sir—well, I can do you blood and love without the rhetoric, and I can do you blood and rhetoric without the love, and I can do you all three concurrent or consecutive, but I can't do you love and rhetoric without the blood. Blood is compulsory—they're all blood, you see.

GUIL: Is that what people want?

PLAYER: It's what we do. (*Small pause. He turns away.*)

GUIL touches ALFRED on the shoulder.

GUIL (*wry, gentle*): Thank you; we'll let you know.

The PLAYER has moved upstage. ALFRED follows.

PLAYER (*to TRAGEDIANS*): Thirty-eight!

ROS (*moving across, fascinated and hopeful*): Position?

PLAYER: Sir?

ROS: One of your—tableaux?

PLAYER: No, sir.

ROS: Oh.

PLAYER (*to the TRAGEDIANS, now departing with their cart, already taking various props off it*): Entrances there and there (*indicating upstage*).

The PLAYER has not moved his position for his last four lines. He does not move now. GUIL waits.

GUIL: Well . . . aren't you going to change into your costume?

PLAYER: I never change out of it, sir.

GUIL: Always in character.

PLAYER: That's it.

> *Pause.*

GUIL: Aren't you going to—come *on*?

PLAYER: I *am* on.

GUIL: But if you *are* on, you can't *come* on. *Can* you?

PLAYER: I *start* on.

GUIL: But it hasn't *started*. Go on. We'll look out for you.

PLAYER: I'll give you a wave.

> *He does not move. His immobility is now pointed, and getting awkward. Pause.* ROS *walks up to him till they are face to face.*

ROS: Excuse me.

> *Pause. The* PLAYER *lifts his downstage foot. It was covering* GUIL'S *coin.* ROS *puts his foot on the coin. Smiles.*

Thank you.

> *The* PLAYER *turns and goes.* ROS *has bent for the coin.*

GUIL (*moving out*): Come on.

ROS: I say—that was lucky.

GUIL (*turning*): What?

ROS: It was tails.

> *He tosses the coin to* GUIL *who catches it. Simultaneously— a lighting change sufficient to alter the exterior mood into interior, but nothing violent.*

> *And* OPHELIA *runs on in some alarm, holding up her skirts— followed by* HAMLET.

OPHELIA *has been sewing and she holds the garment. They are both mute.* HAMLET, *with his doublet all unbraced, no hat upon his head, his stockings fouled, ungartered and down-gyved to his ankle, pale as his shirt, his knees knocking each other . . . and with a look so piteous, he takes her by the wrist and holds her hard, then he goes to the length of his arm, and with his other hand over his brow, falls to such perusal of her face as he would draw it. . . . At last, with a little shaking of his arm, and thrice his head waving up and down, he raises a sigh so piteous and profound that it does seem to shatter all his bulk and end his being. That done he lets her go, and with his head over his shoulder turned, he goes out backwards without taking his eyes off her . . . she runs off in the opposite direction.*

ROS *and* GUIL *have frozen.* GUIL *unfreezes first. He jumps at* ROS.

GUIL: Come on!

But a flourish—enter CLAUDIUS *and* GERTRUDE, *attended.*

CLAUDIUS: Welcome, dear Rosencrantz . . . (*he raises a hand at* GUIL *while* ROS *bows—*GUIL *bows late and hurriedly*) . . . and Guildenstern.

He raises a hand at ROS *while* GUIL *bows to him—*ROS *is still straightening up from his previous bow and halfway up he bows down again. With his head down, he twists to look at* GUIL, *who is on the way up.*

Moreover that we did much long to see you,
The need we have to use you did provoke
Our hasty sending.

ROS *and* GUIL *still adjusting their clothing for* CLAUDIUS's *presence.*

Something have you heard
Of Hamlet's transformation, so call it,

Sith nor th'exterior nor the inward man
Resembles that it was. What it should be,
More than his father's death, that thus hath put him,
So much from th'understanding of himself,
I cannot dream of. I entreat you both
That, being of so young days brought up with him
And sith so neighboured to his youth and haviour
That you vouchsafe your rest here in our court
Some little time, so by your companies
To draw him on to pleasures, and to gather
So much as from occasion you may glean,
Whether aught to us unknown afflicts him thus,
That opened lies within our remedy.

GERTRUDE: Good (*fractional suspense*) gentlemen . . .

They both bow.

He hath much talked of you,
And sure I am, two men there is not living
To whom he more adheres. If it will please you
To show us so much gentry and goodwill
As to expand your time with us awhile
For the supply and profit of our hope,
Your visitation shall receive such thanks
As fits a king's remembrance.

ROS: Both your majesties
Might, by the sovereign power you have of us,
Put your dread pleasures more into command
Than to entreaty.

GUIL: But we both obey,
And here give up ourselves in the full bent
To lay our service freely at your feet,
To be commanded.

CLAUDIUS: Thanks, Rosencrantz (*turning to* ROS *who is caught unprepared, while* GUIL *bows*) and gentle Guildenstern (*turning to* GUIL *who is bent double*).

36

GERTRUDE (*correcting*): Thanks Guildenstern (*turning to* ROS, *who bows as* GUIL *checks upward movement to bow too— both bent double, squinting at each other*) . . . and gentle Rosencrantz (*turning to* GUIL, *both straightening up—*GUIL *checks again and bows again*).

And I beseech you instantly to visit
My too much changed son. Go, some of you,
And bring these gentlemen where Hamlet is.

Two ATTENDANTS *exit backwards, indicating that* ROS *and* GUIL *should follow.*

GUIL: Heaven make our presence and our practices
Pleasant and helpful to him.

GERTRUDE: Ay, amen!

ROS *and* GUIL *move towards a downstage wing. Before they get there,* POLONIUS *enters. They stop and bow to him. He nods and hurries upstage to* CLAUDIUS. *They turn to look at him.*

POLONIUS: The ambassadors from Norway, my good lord, are joyfully returned.

CLAUDIUS: Thou still hast been the father of good news.

POLONIUS: Have I, my lord? Assure you, my good liege,
I hold my duty as I hold my soul,
Both to my God and to my gracious King;
And I do think, or else this brain of mine
Hunts not the trail of policy so sure
As it hath used to do, that I have found
The very cause of Hamlet's lunacy. . . .

Exeunt—leaving ROS *and* GUIL.

ROS: I want to go home.

GUIL: Don't let them confuse you.

ROS: I'm out of my step here——

GUIL: We'll soon be home and high—dry and home—I'll——

ROS: It's all over my *depth*——

GUIL: —I'll hie you home and——

ROS: —out of my head——

GUIL: —dry you high and——

ROS (*cracking, high*): —over my step over my head body!—I tell you it's all stopping to a death, it's boding to a depth, stepping to a head, it's all heading to a dead stop——

GUIL (*the nursemaid*): There! . . . and we'll soon be home and dry . . . and *high* and dry. . . . (*Rapidly.*) Has it ever happened to you that all of a sudden and for no reason at all you haven't the faintest idea how to spell the word—"wife"—or "house"—because when you write it down you just can't remember ever having seen those letters in that order before . . . ?

ROS: I remember——

GUIL: Yes?

ROS: I remember when there were no questions.

GUIL: There were always questions. To exchange one set for another is no great matter.

ROS: Answers, yes. There were answers to everything.

GUIL: You've forgotten.

ROS (*flaring*): I haven't forgotten—how I used to remember my own name—and yours, oh *yes!* There were answers everywhere you *looked*. There was no question about it—people knew who I was and if they didn't they asked and I told them.

GUIL: You did, the trouble is, each of them is . . . plausible, without being instinctive. All your life you live so close to truth, it becomes a permanent blur in the corner of your eye, and when something nudges it into outline it is like being ambushed by a grotesque. A man standing in his saddle in the half-lit half-alive dawn banged on the shutters and called two names. He was just a hat and a cloak levitating in the grey plume of his own breath, but when he called we came. That much is certain—we came.

ROS: Well I can tell you I'm sick to death of it. I don't care one way or another, so why don't you make up your mind.

GUIL: We can't afford anything quite so arbitrary. Nor did we come all this way for a christening. All *that*—preceded us. But we are comparatively fortunate; we might have been left to sift the whole field of human nomenclature, like two blind men looting a bazaar for their own portraits. . . . At least we are presented with alternatives.

ROS: Well as from now——

GUIL: —But not choice.

ROS: You made me look ridiculous in there.

GUIL: I looked just as ridiculous as you did.

ROS (*an anguished cry*): Consistency is all I ask!

GUIL (*low, wry rhetoric*): Give us this day our daily mask.

ROS (*a dying fall*): I want to go home. (*Moves.*) Which way did we come in? I've lost my sense of direction.

GUIL: The only beginning is birth and the only end is death—if you can't count on that, what can you count on?

They connect again.

ROS: We don't owe anything to anyone.

GUIL: We've been caught up. Your smallest action sets off another somewhere else, and is set off by it. Keep an eye

open, an ear cocked. Tread warily, follow instructions.
We'll be all right.

ROS: For how long?

GUIL: Till events have played themselves out. There's a logic at
work—it's all done for you, don't worry. Enjoy it. Relax.
To be taken in hand and led, like being a child again, even
without the innocence, a child—it's like being given a prize,
an extra slice of childhood when you least expect it, as a
prize for being good, or compensation for never having had
one. . . . Do I contradict myself?

ROS: I can't remember. . . . What have we got to go on?

GUIL: We have been briefed. Hamlet's transformation. What do
you recollect?

ROS: Well, he's changed, hasn't he? The exterior and inward
man fails to resemble——

GUIL: Draw him on to pleasures—glean what afflicts him.

ROS: Something more than his father's death——

GUIL: He's always talking about us—there aren't two people
living whom he dotes on more than us.

ROS: We cheer him up—find out what's the matter——

GUIL: Exactly, it's a matter of asking the right questions and
giving away as little as we can. It's a game.

ROS: And then we can go?

GUIL: And receive such thanks as fits a king's remembrance.

ROS: I like the sound of that. What do you think he means by
remembrance?

GUIL: He doesn't forget his friends.

ROS: Would you care to estimate?

GUIL: Difficult to say, really—some kings tend to be amnesiac, others I suppose—the opposite, whatever that is. . . .

ROS: Yes—but——

GUIL: Elephantine . . . ?

ROS: Not how long—how much?

GUIL: *Retentive*—he's a very retentive king, a royal retainer. . . .

ROS: What are you playing at?

GUIL: Words, words. They're all we have to go on.

Pause.

ROS: Shouldn't we be doing something—constructive?

GUIL: What did you have in mind? . . . A short, blunt human pyramid . . . ?

ROS: We could go.

GUIL: Where?

ROS: After him.

GUIL: Why? They've got us placed now—if we start moving around, we'll all be chasing each other all night.

Hiatus.

ROS (*at footlights*): How very intriguing! (*Turns.*) I feel like a spectator—an appalling business. The only thing that makes it bearable is the irrational belief that somebody interesting will come on in a minute. . . .

GUIL: See anyone?

ROS: No. You?

GUIL: No. (*At footlights.*) What a fine persecution—to be kept intrigued without ever quite being enlightened. . . . (*Pause.*) We've had no practice.

ROS: We could play at questions.

GUIL: What good would that do?

ROS: Practice!

GUIL: Statement! One—love.

ROS: Cheating!

GUIL: How?

ROS: I hadn't started yet.

GUIL: Statement. Two—love.

ROS: Are you counting that?

GUIL: What?

ROS: Are you counting that?

GUIL: Foul! No repetitions. Three—love. First game to . . .

ROS: I'm not going to play if you're going to be like that.

GUIL: Whose serve?

ROS: Hah?

GUIL: Foul! No grunts. Love—one.

ROS: Whose go?.

GUIL: Why?

ROS: Why not?

GUIL: What for?

ROS: Foul! No synonyms! One—all.

GUIL: What in God's name is going on?

ROS: Foul! No rhetoric. Two—one.

GUIL: What does it all add up to?

ROS: Can't you guess?

GUIL: Were you addressing me?

ROS: Is there anyone else?

GUIL: Who?

ROS: How would I know?

GUIL: Why do you ask?

ROS: Are you serious?

GUIL: Was that rhetoric?

ROS: No.

GUIL: Statement! Two—all. Game point.

ROS: What's the matter with you today?

GUIL: When?

ROS: What?

GUIL: Are you deaf?

ROS: Am I dead?

GUIL: Yes or no?

ROS: Is there a choice?

GUIL: Is there a God?

ROS: Foul! No *non sequiturs,* three—two, one game all.

GUIL (*seriously*): What's your name?

ROS: What's yours?

GUIL: I asked you first.

ROS: Statement. One—love.

GUIL: What's your name when you're at home?

ROS: What's yours?

GUIL: When I'm at home?

ROS: Is it different at home?

GUIL: What home?

ROS: Haven't you got one?

GUIL: Why do you ask?

ROS: What are you driving at?

GUIL (*with emphasis*): What's your name?!

ROS: Repetition. Two—love. Match point to me.

GUIL (*seizing him violently*): WHO DO YOU THINK YOU ARE?

ROS: Rhetoric! Game and match! (*Pause.*) Where's it going to end?

GUIL: That's the question.

ROS: It's *all* questions.

GUIL: Do you think it matters?

ROS: Doesn't it matter to you ?

GUIL: Why should it matter?

ROS: What does it matter why?

GUIL (*teasing gently*): Doesn't it *matter* why it matters?

ROS (*rounding on him*): What's the *matter* with you?

　　Pause.

GUIL: It doesn't matter.

ROS (*voice in the wilderness*): . . . What's the game?

GUIL: What are the rules?

　　Enter HAMLET *behind, crossing the stage, reading a book—as he is about to disappear* GUIL *notices him.*

GUIL (*sharply*): Rosencrantz!

ROS (*jumps*): What!

> HAMLET *goes. Triumph dawns on them, they smile.*

GUIL: There! How was that?

ROS: Clever!

GUIL: Natural?

ROS: Instinctive.

GUIL: Got it in your head?

ROS: I take my hat off to you.

GUIL: Shake hands.

> *They do.*

ROS: Now I'll try you—Guil—!

GUIL: —Not yet—catch me unawares.

ROS: Right.

> *They separate. Pause. Aside to* GUIL.

Ready?

GUIL (*explodes*): Don't be stupid.

ROS: Sorry.

> *Pause.*

GUIL (*snaps*): Guildenstern!

ROS (*jumps*): What?

> *He is immediately crestfallen,* GUIL *is disgusted.*

GUIL: Consistency is all I ask!

ROS (*quietly*): Immortality is all I seek. . . .

GUIL (*dying fall*): Give us this day our daily week. . . .

> *Beat.*

ROS: Who was that?

GUIL: Didn't you know him?

ROS: He didn't know me.

GUIL: He didn't see you.

ROS: I didn't see him.

GUIL: We shall see. I *hardly* knew him, he's changed.

ROS: You could see that?

GUIL: Transformed.

ROS: How do you know?

GUIL: Inside and out.

ROS: I see.

GUIL: He's not himself.

ROS: He's changed.

GUIL: I could see that.

> *Beat.*

> Glean what afflicts him.

ROS: Me?

GUIL: Him.

ROS: How?

GUIL: Question and answer. Old ways are the best ways.

ROS: He's afflicted.

GUIL: You question, I'll answer.

ROS: He's not himself, you know.

GUIL: I'm him, you see.

> *Beat.*

46

ROS: Who am I then?

GUIL: You're yourself.

ROS: And he's you?

GUIL: Not a bit of it.

ROS: Are you afflicted?

GUIL: That's the idea. Are you ready?

ROS: Let's go back a bit.

GUIL: I'm afflicted.

ROS: I see.

GUIL: Glean what afflicts me.

ROS: Right.

GUIL: Question and answer.

ROS: How should I begin?

GUIL: Address me.

ROS: My dear Guildenstern!

GUIL (*quietly*): You've forgotten—haven't you?

ROS: My dear Rosencrantz!

GUIL (*great control*): I don't think you quite understand. What we are attempting is a hypothesis in which *I* answer for *him*, while *you* ask me questions.

ROS: Ah! Ready?

GUIL: You know what to do?

ROS: What?

GUIL: Are you stupid?

ROS: Pardon?

GUIL: Are you deaf?

ROS: Did you speak?

GUIL (*admonishing*): Not now——

ROS: Statement.

GUIL (*shouts*): Not now! (*Pause.*) If I had any doubts, or rather hopes, they are dispelled. What could we possibly have in common except our situation? (*They separate and sit.*) Perhaps he'll come back this way.

ROS: Should we go?

GUIL: Why?

    Pause.

ROS (*starts up. Snaps fingers*): Oh! You mean—you pretend to be *him,* and *I* ask you questions!

GUIL (*dry*): Very good.

ROS: You had me confused.

GUIL: I could see I had.

ROS: How should I begin?

GUIL: Address me.

    They stand and face each other, posing.

ROS: My honoured Lord!

GUIL: My dear Rosencrantz!

    Pause.

ROS: Am I pretending to be you, then?

GUIL: Certainly not. If you like. Shall we continue?

ROS: Question and answer.

GUIL: Right.

ROS: Right. My honoured lord!

GUIL: My dear fellow!

ROS: How are you?

GUIL: Afflicted!

ROS: Really? In what way?

GUIL: Transformed.

ROS: Inside or out?

GUIL: Both.

ROS: I see. (*Pause.*) Not much new there.

GUIL: Go into details. *Delve.* Probe the background, establish the situation.

ROS: So—so your uncle is the king of Denmark?!

GUIL: And my father before him.

ROS: His father before him?

GUIL: No, my father before him.

ROS: But surely——

GUIL: You might well ask.

ROS: Let me get it straight. Your father was king. You were his only son. Your father dies. You are of age. Your uncle becomes king.

GUIL: Yes.

ROS: Unorthodox.

GUIL: Undid me.

ROS: Undeniable. Where were you?

GUIL: In Germany.

ROS: Usurpation, then.

GUIL: He slipped in.

ROS: Which reminds me.

GUIL: Well, it would.

ROS: I don't want to be personal.

GUIL: It's common knowledge.

ROS: Your mother's marriage.

GUIL: He slipped in.

Beat.

ROS (*lugubriously*): His body was still warm.

GUIL: So was hers.

ROS: Extraordinary.

GUIL: Indecent.

ROS: Hasty.

GUIL: Suspicious.

ROS: It makes you think.

GUIL: Don't think I haven't thought of it.

ROS: And with her husband's brother.

GUIL: They were close.

ROS: She went to him——

GUIL: —Too close——

ROS: —for comfort.

GUIL: It looks bad.

ROS: It adds up.

GUIL: Incest to adultery.

ROS: Would you go so far?

GUIL: Never.

ROS: To sum up: your father, whom you love, dies, you are his heir, you come back to find that hardly was the corpse cold before his young brother popped onto his throne and into his sheets, thereby offending both legal and natural practice. Now why exactly are you behaving in this extraordinary manner?

GUIL: I can't imagine! (*Pause.*) But all that is well known, common property. Yet he sent for us. And we did come.

ROS (*alert, ear cocked*): I say! I heard music——

GUIL: We're here.

ROS: —Like a band—I thought I heard a band.

GUIL: Rosencrantz . . .

ROS (*absently, still listening*): What?

> *Pause, short.*

GUIL (*gently wry*): Guildenstern . . .

ROS (*irritated by the repetition*): *What?*

GUIL: Don't you discriminate at all?

ROS (*turning dumbly*): Wha'?

> *Pause.*

GUIL: Go and see if he's there.

ROS: Who?

GUIL: There.

> ROS *goes to an upstage wing, looks, returns, formally making his report.*

ROS: Yes.

GUIL: What is he doing?

ROS *repeats movement.*

ROS: Talking.

GUIL: To himself?

ROS *starts to move.* GUIL *cuts in impatiently.*

Is he alone?

ROS: No.

GUIL: Then he's not talking to himself, is he?

ROS: Not *by* himself. . . . Coming this way, I think. (*Shiftily.*) Should we go?

GUIL: Why? We're marked now.

HAMLET *enters, backwards, talking, followed by* POLONIUS, *upstage.* ROS *and* GUIL *occupy the two downstage corners looking upstage.*

HAMLET: . . . for you yourself, sir, should be as old as I am if like a crab you could go backward.

POLONIUS (*aside*): Though this be madness, yet there is method in it. Will you walk out of the air, my lord?

HAMLET: Into my grave.

POLONIUS: Indeed, that's out of the air.

HAMLET *crosses to upstage exit,* POLONIUS *asiding unintelligibly until——*

My lord, I will take my leave of you.

HAMLET: You cannot take from me anything that I will more willingly part withal—except my life, except my life, except my life. . . .

POLONIUS (*crossing downstage*): Fare you well, my lord. (*To* ROS:) You go to seek Lord Hamlet? There he is.

ROS (*to* POLONIUS): God save you sir.

POLONIUS *goes.*

GUIL (*calls upstage to* HAMLET): My honoured lord!

ROS: My most dear lord!

    HAMLET *centred upstage, turns to them.*

HAMLET: My excellent good friends! How dost thou Guildenstern? (*Coming downstage with an arm raised to* ROS, GUIL *meanwhile bowing to no greeting.* HAMLET *corrects himself. Still to* ROS:) Ah Rosencrantz!

    They laugh good-naturedly at the mistake. They all meet midstage, turn upstage to walk, HAMLET *in the middle, arm over each shoulder.*

HAMLET: Good lads how do you both?

BLACKOUT

ACT TWO

HAMLET, ROS *and* GUIL *talking, the continuation of the previous scene. Their conversation, on the move, is indecipherable at first. The first intelligible line is* HAMLET's, *coming at the end of a short speech—see Shakespeare Act II, scene ii.*

HAMLET: S'blood, there is something in this more than natural, if philosophy could find it out.

A flourish from the TRAGEDIANS' *band.*

GUIL: There are the players.

HAMLET: Gentlemen, you are welcome to Elsinore. Your hands, come then. (*He takes their hands.*) The appurtenance of welcome is fashion and ceremony. Let me comply with you in this garb, lest my extent to the players (which I tell you must show fairly outwards) should more appear like entertainment than yours. You are welcome. (*About to leave.*) But my uncle-father and aunt-mother are deceived.

GUIL: In what, my dear lord?

HAMLET: I am but mad north north-west; when the wind is southerly I know a hawk from a handsaw.

POLONIUS *enters as* GUIL *turns away.*

POLONIUS: Well be with you gentlemen.

HAMLET (*to* ROS): Mark you, Guildenstern (*uncertainly to* GUIL) and you too; at each ear a hearer. That great baby you see there is not yet out of his swaddling clouts. . . . (*He takes* ROS *upstage with him, talking together.*)

POLONIUS: My Lord! I have news to tell you.

HAMLET (*releasing* ROS *and mimicking*): My lord, I have news to
tell you. . . . When Roscius was an actor in Rome . . .

ROS *comes downstage to rejoin* GUIL.

POLONIUS (*as he follows* HAMLET *out*): The actors are come
hither my lord.

HAMLET: Buzz, buzz.

Exeunt HAMLET *and* POLONIUS.

ROS *and* GUIL *ponder. Each reluctant to speak first.*

GUIL: Hm?

ROS: Yes?

GUIL: What?

ROS: I thought you . . .

GUIL: No.

ROS: Ah.

Pause.

GUIL: I think we can say we made some headway.

ROS: You think so?

GUIL: I think we can say that.

ROS: I think we can say he made us look ridiculous.

GUIL: We played it close to the chest of course.

ROS (*derisively*): "Question and answer. Old ways are the best
ways"! He was scoring off us all down the line.

GUIL: He caught us on the wrong foot once or twice, perhaps,
but I thought we gained some ground.

ROS (*simply*): He murdered us.

GUIL: He might have had the edge.

ROS (*roused*): Twenty-seven—three, and you think he might have had the edge?! He *murdered* us.

GUIL: What about our evasions?

ROS: Oh, our evasions were lovely. "Were you sent for?" he says. "My lord, we were sent for. . . ." I didn't know where to put myself.

GUIL: He had six rhetoricals——

ROS: It was question and answer, all right. Twenty-seven questions he got out in ten minutes, and answered three. I was waiting for you to *delve*. "When is he going to start *delving*?" I asked myself.

GUIL: —And two repetitions.

ROS: Hardly a leading question between us.

GUIL: We got his *symptoms,* didn't we?

ROS: Half of what he said meant something else, and the other half didn't mean anything at all.

GUIL: Thwarted ambition—a sense of grievance, that's my diagnosis.

ROS: Six rhetorical and two repetition, leaving nineteen, of which we answered fifteen. And what did we get in return? He's depressed! . . . Denmark's a prison and he'd rather live in a nutshell; some shadow-play about the nature of ambition, which never got down to cases, and finally one direct question which might have led somewhere, and led in fact to his illuminating claim to tell a hawk from a handsaw.

Pause.

GUIL: When the wind is southerly.

ROS: And the weather's clear.

GUIL: And when it isn't he can't.

ROS: He's at the mercy of the elements. (*Licks his finger and holds it up—facing audience.*) Is that southerly?

They stare at audience.

GUIL: It doesn't *look* southerly. What made you think so?

ROS: I didn't *say* I think so. It could be northerly for all I know.

GUIL: I wouldn't have thought so.

ROS: Well, if you're going to be dogmatic.

GUIL: Wait a minute—we came from roughly south according to a rough map.

ROS: I see. Well, which way did we come in? (GUIL *looks round vaguely.*) Roughly.

GUIL (*clears his throat*): In the morning the sun would be easterly. I think we can assume that.

ROS: That it's morning?

GUIL: If it is, and the sun is over *there* (*his right as he faces the audience*) for instance, *that* (*front*) would be northerly. On the other hand, if it is not morning and the sun is over *there* (*his left*) . . . *that* . . . (*lamely*) would *still* be northerly. (*Picking up.*) To put it another way, if we came from down there (*front*) and it is morning, the sun would be up there (*his left*), and if it is actually over *there* (*his right*) and it's still morning, we must have come from up *there* (*behind him*), and if *that* is southerly (*his left*) and the sun is really over *there* (*front*), then it's the afternoon. However, if none of these is the case——

ROS: Why don't you go and have a look?

GUIL: Pragmatism?!—is that all you have to offer? You seem to have no conception of where we stand! You won't find the answer written down for you in the bowl of a compass

58

—I can tell you that. (*Pause.*) Besides, you can never tell this far north—it's probably dark out there.

ROS: I merely suggest that the position of the sun, if it is out, would give you a rough idea of the time; alternatively, the clock, if it is going, would give you a rough idea of the position of the sun. I forget which you're trying to establish.

GUIL: I'm trying to establish the direction of the wind.

ROS: There isn't any wind. *Draught,* yes.

GUIL: In that case, the origin. Trace it to its source and it might give us a rough idea of the way we came in—which might give us a rough idea of south, for further reference.

ROS: It's coming up through the floor. (*He studies the floor.*) That can't be south, can it?

GUIL: That's not a direction. Lick your toe and wave it around a bit.

ROS *considers the distance of his foot.*

ROS: No, I think you'd have to lick it for me.

Pause.

GUIL: I'm prepared to let the whole matter drop.

ROS: Or I could lick yours, of course.

GUIL: No thank you.

ROS: I'll even wave it around for you.

GUIL (*down* ROS's *throat*): What in God's name is the matter with you?

ROS: Just being friendly.

GUIL (*retiring*): Somebody might come in. It's what we're counting on, after all. Ultimately.

Good pause.

ROS: Perhaps they've all trampled each other to death in the rush. . . . Give them a shout. Something provocative. *Intrigue* them.

GUIL: Wheels have been set in motion, and they have their own pace, to which we are . . . condemned. Each move is dictated by the previous one—that is the meaning of order. If we start being arbitrary it'll just be a shambles: at least, let us hope so. Because if we happened, just happened to discover, or even suspect, that our spontaneity was part of their order, we'd know that we were lost. (*He sits.*) A Chinaman of the T'ang Dynasty—and, by which definition, a philosopher—dreamed he was a butterfly, and from that moment he was never quite sure that he was not a butterfly dreaming it was a Chinese philosopher. Envy him; in his two-fold security.

A good pause. ROS *leaps up and bellows at the audience.*

ROS: Fire!

GUIL *jumps up.*

GUIL: Where?

ROS: It's all right—I'm demonstrating the misuse of free speech. To prove that it exists. (*He regards the audience, that is the direction, with contempt—and other directions, then front again.*) Not a move. They should burn to death in their shoes. (*He takes out one of his coins. Spins it. Catches it. Looks at it. Replaces it.*)

GUIL: What was it?

ROS: What?

GUIL: Heads or tails?

ROS: Oh. I didn't look.

GUIL: Yes you did.

ROS: Oh, did I? (*He takes out a coin, studies it.*) Quite right—
it rings a bell.

GUIL: What's the last thing you remember?

ROS: I don't wish to be reminded of it.

GUIL: We cross our bridges when we come to them and burn
them behind us, with nothing to show for our progress
except a memory of the smell of smoke, and a presumption
that once our eyes watered.

*ROS approaches him brightly, holding a coin between finger
and thumb. He covers it with his other hand, draws his fists
apart and holds them for GUIL. GUIL considers them. Indicates
the left hand, ROS opens it to show it empty.*

ROS: No.

*Repeat process. GUIL indicates left hand again. ROS shows it
empty.*

Double bluff!

*Repeat process—GUIL taps one hand, then the other hand,
quickly. ROS inadvertently shows that both are empty. ROS
laughs as GUIL turns upstage. ROS stops laughing, looks
around his feet, pats his clothes, puzzled.*

*POLONIUS breaks that up by entering upstage followed by the
TRAGEDIANS and HAMLET.*

POLONIUS (*entering*): Come sirs.

HAMLET: Follow him, friends. We'll hear a play tomorrow.
(*Aside to the PLAYER, who is the last of the TRAGEDIANS:*)
Dost thou hear me, old friend? Can you play *The Murder
of Gonzago*?

PLAYER: Ay, my lord.

HAMLET: We'll ha't tomorrow night. You could for a need study a speech of some dozen or sixteen lines which I would set down and insert in't, could you not?

PLAYER: Ay, my lord.

HAMLET: Very well. Follow that lord, and look you mock him not.

The PLAYER *crossing downstage, notes* ROS *and* GUIL. *Stops.* HAMLET *crossing downstage addresses them without pause.*

HAMLET: My good friends, I'll leave you till tonight. You are welcome to Elsinore.

ROS: Good, my lord.

HAMLET *goes.*

GUIL: So you've caught up.

PLAYER (*coldly*): Not yet, sir.

GUIL: Now mind your tongue, or we'll have it out and throw the rest of you away, like a nightingale at a Roman feast.

ROS: Took the very words out of my mouth.

GUIL: You'd be *lost* for words.

ROS: You'd be tongue-tied.

GUIL: Like a mute in a monologue.

ROS: Like a nightingale at a Roman feast.

GUIL: Your diction will go to pieces.

ROS: Your lines will be cut.

GUIL: To dumbshows.

ROS: And dramatic pauses.

GUIL: You'll never *find* your tongue.

ROS: Lick your lips.

GUIL: Taste your tears.

ROS: Your breakfast.

GUIL: You won't know the difference.

ROS: There won't be any.

GUIL: We'll take the very words out of your mouth.

ROS: So you've caught on.

GUIL: So you've caught up.

PLAYER (*tops*): Not yet! (*Bitterly.*) You left us.

GUIL: Ah! I'd forgotten—you performed a dramatic spectacle
on the way. Yes, I'm sorry we had to miss it.

PLAYER (*bursts out*): We can't look each other in the face! (*Pause,
more in control.*) You don't understand the humiliation of it
—to be tricked out of the single assumption which makes our
existence viable—that somebody is *watching*. . . . The plot
was two corpses gone before we caught sight of ourselves,
stripped naked in the middle of nowhere and pouring
ourselves down a bottomless well.

ROS: Is *that* thirty-eight?

PLAYER (*lost*): There we were—demented children mincing about
in clothes that no one ever wore, speaking as no man ever
spoke, swearing love in wigs and rhymed couplets, killing
each other with wooden swords, hollow protestations of
faith hurled after empty promises of vengeance—and every
gesture, every pose, vanishing into the thin unpopulated air.
We ransomed our dignity to the clouds, and the uncompre-
hending birds listened. (*He rounds on them.*) Don't you
see?! We're *actors*—we're the opposite of people! (*They
recoil nonplussed, his voice calms.*) Think, in your head,
now, think of the most . . . *private* . . . *secret* . . . *intimate*

63

thing you have ever done secure in the knowledge of its privacy. . . . (*He gives them—and the audience—a good pause.* ROS *takes on a shifty look.*) Are you thinking of it? (*He strikes with his voice and his head.*) *Well, I saw you do it!*

ROS *leaps up, dissembling madly.*

ROS: You never! It's a lie! (*He catches himself with a giggle in a vacuum and sits down again.*)

PLAYER: We're actors. . . . We pledged our identities, secure in the conventions of our trade, that someone would be watching. And then, gradually, no one was. We were caught, high and dry. It was not until the murderer's long soliloquy that we were able to look around; frozen as we were in profile, our eyes searched you out, first confidently, then hesitantly, then desperately as each patch of turf, each log, every exposed corner in every direction proved uninhabited, and all the while the murderous King addressed the horizon with his dreary interminable guilt. . . . Our heads began to move, wary as lizards, the corpse of unsullied Rosalinda peeped through his fingers, and the King faltered. Even then, habit and a stubborn trust that our audience spied upon us from behind the nearest bush, forced our bodies to blunder on long after they had emptied of meaning, until like runaway carts they dragged to a halt. No one came forward. No one shouted at us. The silence was unbreakable, it imposed itself upon us; it was obscene. We took off our crowns and swords and cloth of gold and moved silent on the road to Elsinore.

Silence. Then GUIL *claps solo with slow measured irony.*

GUIL: Brilliantly re-created—if these eyes could weep! . . . Rather strong on metaphor, mind you. No criticism—only a matter of taste. And so here you are—with a vengeance. That's a figure of speech . . . isn't it? Well let's say we've made up for it, for you may have no doubt whom to thank for your performance at the court.

ROS: We are counting on you to take him out of himself. You are the pleasures which we draw him on to—(*he escapes a fractional giggle but recovers immediately*) and by that I don't mean your usual filth; you can't treat royalty like people with normal perverted desires. They know nothing of that and you know nothing of them, to your mutual survival. So give him a good clean show suitable for all the family, or you can rest assured you'll be playing the tavern tonight.

GUIL: Or the night after.

ROS: Or not.

PLAYER: We already have an entry here. And always have had.

GUIL: You've played for him before?

PLAYER: Yes, sir.

ROS: And what's *his* bent?

PLAYER: Classical.

ROS: Saucy!

GUIL: What will you play?

PLAYER: *The Murder of Gonzago.*

GUIL: Full of fine cadence and corpses.

PLAYER: Pirated from the Italian. . . .

ROS: What is it about?

PLAYER: It's about a King and Queen. . . .

GUIL: Escapism! What else?

PLAYER: Blood——

GUIL: —Love and rhetoric.

PLAYER: Yes. (*Going.*)

GUIL: Where are you going?

PLAYER: I can come and go as I please.

GUIL: You're evidently a man who knows his way around.

PLAYER: I've been here before.

GUIL: We're still finding our feet.

PLAYER: I should concentrate on not losing your heads.

GUIL: Do you speak from knowledge?

PLAYER: Precedent.

GUIL: You've been here before.

PLAYER: And I know which way the wind is blowing.

GUIL: Operating on two levels, are we?! How clever! I expect it comes naturally to you, being in the business so to speak.

The PLAYER's *grave face does not change. He makes to move off again.* GUIL *for the second time cuts him off.*

The truth is, we value your company, for want of any other. We have been left so much to our own devices— after a while one welcomes the uncertainty of being left to other people's.

PLAYER: Uncertainty is the normal state. You're nobody special.

He makes to leave again. GUIL *loses his cool.*

GUIL: But for God's sake what are we supposed to *do*?!

PLAYER: Relax. Respond. That's what people do. You can't go through life questioning your situation at every turn.

GUIL: But we don't know what's going on, or what to do with ourselves. We don't know how to *act*.

PLAYER: Act natural. You know why you're here at least.

GUIL: We only know what we're told, and that's little enough. And for all we know it isn't even true.

PLAYER: For all anyone knows, nothing is. Everything has to be taken on trust; truth is only that which is taken to be true. It's the currency of living. There may be nothing behind it, but it doesn't make any difference so long as it is honoured. One acts on assumptions. What do you assume?

ROS: Hamlet is not himself, outside or in. We have to glean what afflicts him.

GUIL: He doesn't give much away.

PLAYER: Who does, nowadays?

GUIL: He's—melancholy.

PLAYER: Melancholy?

ROS: Mad.

PLAYER: How is he mad?

ROS: Ah. (*To* GUIL:) How is he mad?

GUIL: More morose than mad, perhaps.

PLAYER: Melancholy.

GUIL: Moody.

ROS: He has moods.

PLAYER: Of moroseness?

GUIL: Madness. And yet.

ROS: Quite.

GUIL: For instance.

ROS: He talks to himself, which might be madness.

GUIL: If he didn't talk sense, which he does.

ROS: Which suggests the opposite.

PLAYER: Of what?

Small pause.

GUIL: I think I have it. A man talking sense to himself is no madder than a man talking nonsense not to himself.

ROS: Or just as mad.

GUIL: Or just as mad.

ROS: And he does both.

GUIL: So there you are.

ROS: Stark raving sane.

Pause.

PLAYER: Why?

GUIL: Ah. (*To* ROS:) Why?

ROS: Exactly.

GUIL: Exactly what?

ROS: Exactly why.

GUIL: Exactly why *what*?

ROS: What?

GUIL: *Why?*

ROS: Why what, exactly?

GUIL: Why is he mad?!

ROS: *I* don't know!

Beat.

PLAYER: The old man thinks he's in love with his daughter.

ROS (*appalled*): Good God! We're out of our depth here.

68

PLAYER: No, no, no—*he* hasn't got a daughter—the old man thinks he's in love with *his* daughter.

ROS: The old man is?

PLAYER: Hamlet, in love with the old man's daughter, the old man thinks.

ROS: Ha! It's beginning to make sense! Unrequited passion!

The PLAYER *moves.*

GUIL: (*Fascist.*) Nobody leaves this room! (*Pause, lamely.*) Without a *very* good reason.

PLAYER: Why not?

GUIL: All this strolling about is getting too arbitrary by half—I'm rapidly losing my grip. From now on reason will prevail.

PLAYER: I have lines to learn.

GUIL: Pass!

The PLAYER *passes into one of the wings.* ROS *cups his hands and shouts into the opposite one.*

ROS: Next!

But no one comes.

GUIL: What did you expect?

ROS: Something . . . someone . . . nothing.

They sit facing front.

Are you hungry?

GUIL: No, are you?

ROS (*thinks*): No. You remember that coin?

GUIL: No.

69

ROS: I think I lost it.

GUIL: What coin?

ROS: I don't remember exactly.

Pause.

GUIL: Oh, that coin . . . clever.

ROS: I can't remember how I did it.

GUIL: It probably comes natural to you.

ROS: Yes, I've got a show-stopper there.

GUIL: Do it again.

Slight pause.

ROS: We can't afford it.

GUIL: Yes, one must think of the future.

ROS: It's the normal thing.

GUIL: To have one. One is, after all, having it all the time . . . now . . . and now . . . and now. . . .

ROS: It could go on for ever. Well, not for *ever,* I suppose. (*Pause.*) Do you ever think of yourself as actually *dead,* lying in a box with a lid on it?

GUIL: No.

ROS: Nor do I, really. . . . It's silly to be depressed by it. I mean one thinks of it like being *alive* in a box, one keeps forgetting to take into account the fact that one is *dead* . . . which should make all the difference . . . shouldn't it? I mean, you'd never *know* you were in a box, would you? It would be just like being *asleep* in a box. Not that I'd like to sleep in a box, mind you, not without any air—you'd wake up dead, for a start, and then where would you be? Apart from inside a box. That's the bit I don't like, frankly. That's why I don't think of it. . . .

GUIL *stirs restlessly, pulling his cloak round him.*

Because you'd be helpless, wouldn't you? Stuffed in a box like that, I mean you'd be in there for ever. Even taking into account the fact that you're dead, it isn't a pleasant thought. *Especially* if you're dead, really . . . *ask* yourself, if I asked you straight off—I'm going to stuff you in this box now, would you rather be alive or dead? Naturally, you'd prefer to be alive. Life in a box is better than no life at all. I expect. You'd have a chance at least. You could lie there thinking— well, at least I'm not dead! In a minute someone's going to bang on the lid and tell me to come out. (*Banging the floor with his fists.*) "Hey you, whatsyername! Come out of there!"

GUIL (*jumps up savagely*): You don't have to flog it to death!

Pause.

ROS: I wouldn't think about it, if I were you. You'd only get depressed. (*Pause.*) Eternity is a terrible thought. I mean, where's it going to end? (*Pause, then brightly.*) Two early Christians chanced to meet in Heaven. "Saul of Tarsus yet!" cried one. "What are *you* doing here?!" . . . "Tarsus-Schmarsus," replied the other, "I'm Paul already." (*He stands up restlessly and flaps his arms.*) They don't care. We count for nothing. We could remain silent till we're green in the face, they wouldn't come.

GUIL: Blue, red.

ROS: A Christian, a Moslem and a Jew chanced to meet in a closed carriage. . . . "Silverstein!" cried the Jew. "Who's your friend?" . . . "His name's Abdullah," replied the Moslem, "but he's no friend of mine since he became a convert." (*He leaps up again, stamps his foot and shouts into the wings.*) All right, we know you're in there! Come out talking! (*Pause.*) We have no control. None at all . . . (*He paces.*) Whatever became of the moment when one first knew about death? There must have been one, a moment,

71

in childhood when it first occurred to you that you don't go on for ever. It must have been shattering—stamped into one's memory. And yet I can't remember it. It never occurred to me at all. What does one make of that? We must be born with an intuition of mortality. Before we know the words for it, before we know that there are words, out we come, bloodied and squalling with the knowledge that for all the compasses in the world, there's only one direction, and time is its only measure. (*He reflects, getting more desperate and rapid.*) A Hindu, a Buddhist and a lion-tamer chanced to meet, in a circus on the Indo-Chinese border. (*He breaks out.*) They're taking us for granted! Well, I won't stand for it! In future, notice will be taken. (*He wheels again to face into the wings.*) Keep out, then! I forbid anyone to enter! (*No one comes. Breathing heavily.*) That's better. . . .

Immediately, behind him a grand procession enters, principally CLAUDIUS, GERTRUDE, POLONIUS *and* OPHELIA. CLAUDIUS *takes* ROS's *elbow as he passes and is immediately deep in conversation: the context is Shakespeare Act III, scene i.* GUIL *still faces front as* CLAUDIUS, ROS, *etc., pass upstage and turn.*

GUIL: Death followed by eternity . . . the worst of both worlds. It *is* a terrible thought.

He turns upstage in time to take over the conversation with CLAUDIUS. GERTRUDE *and* ROS *head downstage.*

GERTRUDE: Did he receive you well?

ROS: Most like a gentleman.

GUIL (*returning in time to take it up*): But with much forcing of his disposition.

ROS (*a flat lie and he knows it and shows it, perhaps catching* GUIL's *eye*): Niggard of question, but of our demands most free in his reply.

GERTRUDE: Did you assay him to any pastime?

ROS: Madam, it so fell out that certain players
   We o'erraught on the way: of these we told him
   And there did seem in him a kind of joy
   To hear of it. They are here about the court,
   And, as I think, they have already order
   This night to play before him.

POLONIUS: 'Tis most true
   And he beseeched me to entreat your Majesties
   To hear and see the matter.

CLAUDIUS: With all my heart, and it doth content me
   To hear him so inclined.
   Good gentlemen, give him a further edge
   And drive his purpose into these delights.

ROS: We shall, my lord.

CLAUDIUS (*leading out procession*):
   Sweet Gertrude, leave us, too,
   For we have closely sent for Hamlet hither,
   That he, as t'were by accident, may here
   Affront Ophelia. . . .

   Exeunt CLAUDIUS *and* GERTRUDE.

ROS (*peevish*): Never a moment's peace! In and out, on and off,
   they're coming at us from all sides.

GUIL: You're never satisfied.

ROS: Catching us on the trot. . . . Why can't *we* go by *them*?

GUIL: What's the difference?

ROS: I'm going.

   ROS *pulls his cloak round him.* GUIL *ignores him. Without
   confidence* ROS *heads upstage. He looks out and comes back
   quickly.*

73

He's coming.

GUIL: What's he doing?

ROS: Nothing.

GUIL: He must be doing something.

ROS: Walking.

GUIL: On his hands?

ROS: No, on his feet.

GUIL: Stark naked?

ROS: Fully dressed.

GUIL: Selling toffee apples?

ROS: Not that I noticed.

GUIL: You could be wrong?

ROS: I don't think so.

Pause.

GUIL: I can't for the life of me see how we're going to get into conversation.

HAMLET *enters upstage, and pauses, weighing up the pros and cons of making his quietus.*

ROS *and* GUIL *watch him.*

ROS: Nevertheless, I suppose one might say that this was a chance. . . . One might well . . . accost him. . . . Yes, it definitely looks like a chance to me. . . . Something on the lines of a direct informal approach . . . man to man . . . straight from the shoulder. . . . Now look here, what's it all about . . . sort of thing. Yes. Yes, this looks like one to be grabbed with both hands, I should say . . . if I were asked. . . . No point in looking at a gift horse till you see the whites of its eyes, etcetera. (*He has moved towards* HAMLET

74

but his nerve fails. He returns.) We're overawed, that's our trouble. When it comes to the point we succumb to their personality. . . .

OPHELIA enters, with prayerbook, a religious procession of one.

HAMLET: Nymph, in thy orisons be all my sins remembered.

At his voice she has stopped for him, he catches her up.

OPHELIA: Good my lord, how does your honour for this many a day?

HAMLET: I humbly thank you—well, well, well.

They disappear talking into the wing.

ROS: It's like living in a public park!

GUIL: Very impressive. Yes, I thought your direct informal approach was going to stop this thing dead in its tracks there. If I might make a suggestion—shut up and sit down. Stop being perverse.

ROS (*near tears*): I'm not going to stand for it!

A FEMALE FIGURE, ostensibly the QUEEN, enters. ROS marches up behind her, puts his hands over her eyes and says with a desperate frivolity.

ROS: Guess who?!

PLAYER (*having appeared in a downstage corner*): Alfred!

ROS lets go, spins around. He has been holding ALFRED, in his robe and blond wig. PLAYER is in the downstage corner still. ROS comes down to that exit. The PLAYER does not budge. He and ROS stand toe to toe.

ROS: Excuse me.

The PLAYER lifts his downstage foot. ROS bends to put his

hand on the floor. The PLAYER *lowers his foot.* ROS *screams and leaps away.*

PLAYER (*gravely*): I beg your pardon.

GUIL (*to* ROS): What did he do?

PLAYER: I put my foot down.

ROS: My hand was on the floor!

GUIL: You put your hand under his foot?

ROS: I——

GUIL: What for?

ROS: I thought—— (*Grabs* GUIL.) Don't leave me!

He makes a break for an exit. A TRAGEDIAN *dressed as a* KING *enters.* ROS *recoils, breaks for the opposite wing. Two cloaked* TRAGEDIANS *enter.* ROS *tries again but another* TRAGEDIAN *enters, and* ROS *retires to midstage. The* PLAYER *claps his hands matter-of-factly.*

PLAYER: Right! We haven't got much time.

GUIL: What are you doing?

PLAYER: Dress rehearsal. Now if you two wouldn't mind just moving back . . . there . . . good. . . . (*To* TRAGEDIANS.*) Everyone ready? And for goodness' sake, remember what we're doing. (*To* ROS *and* GUIL:) We always use the same costumes more or less, and they forget what they are supposed to be *in* you see. . . . Stop picking your nose, Alfred. When Queens have to they do it by a cerebral process passed down in the blood. . . . Good. Silence! Off we go!

PLAYER-KING: Full thirty times hath Phoebus' cart——

PLAYER *jumps up angrily.*

PLAYER: No, no, no! Dumbshow first, your confounded majesty!

76

(*To* ROS *and* GUIL:) They're a bit out of practice, but they always pick up wonderfully for the deaths—it brings out the poetry in them.

GUIL: How nice.

PLAYER: There's nothing more unconvincing than an unconvincing death.

GUIL: I'm sure.

> PLAYER *claps his hands.*

PLAYER: Act One—moves now.

> *The mime. Soft music from a recorder.* PLAYER-KING *and* PLAYER-QUEEN *embrace. She kneels and makes a show of protestation to him. He takes her up, declining his head upon her neck. He lies down. She, seeing him asleep, leaves him.*

GUIL: What is the dumbshow for?

PLAYER: Well, it's a device, really—it makes the action that follows more or less comprehensible; you understand, we are tied down to a language which makes up in obscurity what it lacks in style.

> *The mime* (*continued*)—*enter another. He takes off the* SLEEPER'*s crown, kisses it. He has brought in a small bottle of liquid. He pours the poison in the* SLEEPER'*s ear, and leaves him. The* SLEEPER *convulses heroically, dying.*

ROS: Who was that?

PLAYER: The King's brother and uncle to the Prince.

GUIL: Not exactly fraternal

PLAYER: Not exactly avuncular, as time goes on.

> *The* QUEEN *returns, makes passionate action, finding the* KING *dead. The* POISONER *comes in again, attended by two*

77

others (the two in cloaks). The POISONER *seems to console with
her. The dead body is carried away. The* POISONER *woos the*
QUEEN *with gifts. She seems harsh awhile but in the end
accepts his love. End of mime, at which point, the wail of a
woman in torment and* OPHELIA *appears, wailing, closely
followed by* HAMLET *in a hysterical state, shouting at her,
circling her, both midstage.*

HAMLET: Go to, I'll no more on't; it hath made me mad!

She falls on her knees weeping.

I say we will have no more marriage! (*His voice drops to
include the* TRAGEDIANS, *who have frozen.*) Those that are
married already (*he leans close to the* PLAYER-QUEEN *and*
POISONER, *speaking with quiet edge*) all but one shall live.
(*He smiles briefly at them without mirth, and starts to back
out, his parting shot rising again.*) The rest shall keep as they
are. (*As he leaves,* OPHELIA *tottering upstage, he speaks into
her ear a quick clipped sentence.*) To a nunnery, go.

He goes out. OPHELIA *falls on to her knees upstage, her sobs
barely audible. A slight silence.*

PLAYER-KING: Full thirty times hath Phoebus' cart——

CLAUDIUS *enters with* POLONIUS *and goes over to* OPHELIA
and lifts her to her feet. The TRAGEDIANS *jump back with
heads inclined.*

CLAUDIUS: Love? His affections do not that way tend,
Or what he spake, though it lacked form a little,
Was not like madness. There's something
In his soul o'er which his melancholy sits on
Brood, and I do doubt the hatch and the
Disclose will be some danger; which for to
Prevent I have in quick determination thus set
It down: he shall with speed to England . . .

Which carries the three of them—CLAUDIUS, POLONIUS,

78

OPHELIA—*out of sight. The* PLAYER *moves, clapping his hands for attention.*

PLAYER: Gentle*men*! (*They look at him.*) It doesn't seem to be coming. We are not getting it at all. (*To* GUIL:) What did you think?

GUIL: What was I supposed to think?

PLAYER (*to* TRAGEDIANS): You're not getting across!

ROS *had gone halfway up to* OPHELIA; *he returns.*

ROS: That didn't look like love to me.

GUIL: Starting from scratch again . . .

PLAYER (*to* TRAGEDIANS): It was a *mess.*

ROS (*to* GUIL): It's going to be chaos on the night.

GUIL: Keep back—we're spectators.

PLAYER: Act Two! Positions!

GUIL: Wasn't that the end?

PLAYER: Do you call that an ending?—with practically everyone on his feet? My goodness no—over your dead body.

GUIL: How am I supposed to take that?

PLAYER: Lying down. (*He laughs briefly and in a second has never laughed in his life.*) There's a design at work in all art—surely you know that? Events must play themselves out to aesthetic, moral and logical conclusion.

GUIL: And what's that, in this case? *does this play really end that*

PLAYER: It never varies—we aim at the point where everyone *way.* who is marked for death dies.

GUIL: Marked?

PLAYER: Between "just desserts" and "tragic irony" we are given quite a lot of scope for our particular talent.

79

Generally speaking, things have gone about as far as they can possibly go when things have got about as bad as they reasonably get. (*He switches on a smile.*)

GUIL: Who decides?

PLAYER (*switching off his smile*): Decides? It is written. (B+ SHAKESPEARE)

He turns away. GUIL *grabs him and spins him back violently.*

(*Unflustered.*) Now if you're going to be subtle, we'll miss each other in the dark. I'm referring to oral tradition. So to speak.

GUIL *releases him.*

Wilde {We're tragedians, you see. We follow directions—there is no choice involved. The bad end unhappily, the good unluckily. That is what tragedy means. (*Calling.*) Positions!

The TRAGEDIANS *have taken up positions for the continuation of the mime: which in this case means a love scene, sexual and passionate, between the* QUEEN *and the* POISONER/KING.

PLAYER: Go!

The lovers begin. The PLAYER *contributes a breathless commentary for* ROS *and* GUIL.

Having murdered his brother and wooed the widow—the poisoner mounts the throne! Here we see him and his queen give rein to their unbridled passion! She little knowing that the man she holds in her arms——!

ROS: Oh, I say—here—really! You can't do that!

PLAYER: Why not?

ROS: Well, really—I mean, people want to be *entertained*—they don't come expecting sordid and gratuitous filth.

PLAYER: You're wrong—they do! Murder, seduction and incest—what do you want—jokes?

ROS: I want a good story, with a beginning, middle and end.

80

PLAYER (*to* GUIL): And you?

GUIL: I'd prefer art to mirror life, if it's all the same to you.

PLAYER: It's all the same to me, sir. (*To the grappling* LOVERS:) All right, no need to indulge yourselves. (*They get up. To* GUIL:) I come on in a minute. Lucianus, nephew to the king! (*Turns his attention to the* TRAGEDIANS.) Next!

They disport themselves to accommodate the next piece of mime, which consists of the PLAYER *himself exhibiting an excitable anguish* (*choreographed, stylized*) *leading to an impassioned scene with the* QUEEN (*cf. "The Closet Scene," Shakespeare Act III, scene iv*) *and a very stylized reconstruction of a* POLONIUS *figure being stabbed behind the arras* (*the murdered* KING *to stand in for* POLONIUS) *while the* PLAYER *himself continues his breathless commentary for the benefit of* ROS *and* GUIL.

PLAYER: Lucianus, nephew to the king . . . usurped by his uncle and shattered by his mother's incestuous marriage . . . loses his reason . . . throwing the court into turmoil and disarray as he alternates between bitter melancholy and unrestricted lunacy . . . staggering from the suicidal (*a pose*) to the homicidal (*here he kills* "POLONIUS") . . . he at last confronts his mother and in a scene of provocative ambiguity—(*a somewhat oedipal embrace*) begs her to repent and recant—— (*He springs up, still talking.*) The King—(*he pushes forward the* POISONER/KING) tormented by guilt—haunted by fear —decides to despatch his nephew to England—and entrusts this undertaking to two smiling accomplices—friends— courtiers—to two spies——

He has swung round to bring together the POISONER/KING *and the two cloaked* TRAGEDIANS; *the latter kneel and accept a scroll from the* KING.

—giving them a letter to present to the English court——! And so they depart—on board ship——

The two SPIES *position themselves on either side of the* PLAYER, *and the three of them sway gently in unison, the motion of a boat; and then the* PLAYER *detaches himself.*

—and they arrive——

One SPY *shades his eyes at the horizon.*

—and disembark—and present themselves before the English king——(*He wheels round.*) The English king——

An exchange of headgear creates the ENGLISH KING *from the remaining player—that is, the* PLAYER *who played the original murdered king.*

But where is the Prince? Where indeed? The plot has thickened—a twist of fate and cunning has put into their hands a letter that seals their deaths!

The two SPIES *present their letter; the* ENGLISH KING *reads it and orders their deaths. They stand up as the* PLAYER *whips off their cloaks preparatory to execution.*

Traitors hoist by their own petard?—or victims of the gods? —we shall never know!

The whole mime has been fluid and continuous but now ROS *moves forward and brings it to a pause. What brings* ROS *forward is the fact that under their cloaks the two* SPIES *are wearing coats identical to those worn by* ROS *and* GUIL, *whose coats are now covered by their cloaks.* ROS *approaches "his"* SPY *doubtfully. He does not quite understand why the coats are familiar.* ROS *stands close, touches the coat, thoughtfully. . . .*

ROS: Well, if it isn't——! No, wait a minute, don't tell me—it's a long time since—where was it? Ah, this is taking me back to—when was it? I know you, don't I? I never forget a face—(*he looks into the* SPY's *face*) . . . not that I know yours, that is. For a moment I thought—no, I don't know you, do I? Yes, I'm afraid you're quite wrong. You must have mistaken me for someone else.

GUIL *meanwhile has approached the other* SPY, *brow creased in thought.*

PLAYER (*to* GUIL): Are you familiar with this play?

GUIL: No.

PLAYER: A slaughterhouse—eight corpses all told. It brings out the best in us.

GUIL (*tense, progressively rattled during the whole mime and commentary*): You!—What do *you* know about *death*?

PLAYER: It's what the actors do best. They have to exploit whatever talent is given to them, and their talent is dying. They can die heroically, comically, ironically, slowly, suddenly, disgustingly, charmingly, or from a great height. My own talent is more general. I extract significance from melodrama, a significance which it does not in fact contain; but occasionally, from out of this matter, there escapes a thin beam of light that, seen at the right angle, can crack the shell of mortality.

ROS: Is that all they can do—die?

PLAYER: No, no—they kill beautifully. In fact some of them kill even better than they die. The rest die better than they kill. They're a team.

ROS: Which ones are which?

PLAYER: There's not much in it.

GUIL (*fear, derision*): Actors! The mechanics of cheap melodrama! That isn't *death*! (*More quietly.*) You scream and choke and sink to your knees, but it doesn't bring death home to anyone—it doesn't catch them unawares and start the whisper in their skulls that says—"One day you are going to die." (*He straightens up.*) You die so many times; how can you expect them to believe in your death?

PLAYER: On the contrary, it's the only kind they do believe.

They're conditioned to it. I had an actor once who was condemned to hang for stealing a sheep—or a lamb, I forget which—so I got permission to have him hanged in the middle of a play—had to change the plot a bit but I thought it would be effective, you know—and you wouldn't believe it, he just *wasn't* convincing! It was impossible to suspend one's disbelief—and what with the audience jeering and throwing peanuts, the whole thing was a *disaster!*—he did nothing but cry all the time—right out of character—just stood there and cried. . . . Never again.

In good humour he has already turned back to the mime: the two SPIES *awaiting execution at the hands of the* PLAYER, *who takes his dagger out of his belt.*

Audiences know what to expect, and that is all that they are prepared to believe in. (*To the* SPIES:) Show!

The SPIES *die at some length, rather well.*

The light has begun to go, and it fades as they die, and as GUIL *speaks.*

GUIL: No, no, no . . . you've got it all wrong . . . you can't act death. The *fact* of it is nothing to do with seeing it happen —it's not gasps and blood and falling about—that isn't what makes it death. It's just a man failing to reappear, that's all —now you see him, now you don't, that's the only thing that's real: here one minute and gone the next and never coming back—an exit, unobtrusive and unannounced, a disappearance gathering weight as it goes on, until, finally, it is heavy with death.

The two SPIES *lie still, barely visible. The* PLAYER *comes forward and throws the* SPIES' *cloaks over their bodies.* ROS *starts to clap, slowly.*

BLACKOUT.

A second of silence, then much noise. Shouts . . . "The King

rises!" . . . "Give o'er the play!" . . . and cries for "Lights,
lights, lights!"

When the light comes, after a few seconds, it comes as a
sunrise.

The stage is empty save for two cloaked figures sprawled on
the ground in the approximate positions last held by the dead
SPIES. As the light grows, they are seen to be ROS *and* GUIL,
and to be resting quite comfortably. ROS *raises himself on his*
elbows and shades his eyes as he stares into the auditorium.
Finally:

ROS: That must be east, then. I think we can assume that.

GUIL: I'm assuming nothing.

ROS: No, it's all right. That's the sun. East.

GUIL (*looks up*): Where?

ROS: I watched it come up.

GUIL: No . . . it was light all the time, you see, and you opened
    your eyes very, very slowly. If you'd been facing back there
    you'd be swearing *that* was east.

ROS (*standing up*): You're a mass of prejudice.

GUIL: I've been taken in before.

ROS (*looks out over the audience*): Rings a bell.

GUIL: They're waiting to see what we're going to do.

ROS: Good old east.

GUIL: As soon as we make a move they'll come pouring in from
    every side, shouting obscure instructions, confusing us with
    ridiculous remarks, messing us about from here to
    breakfast and getting our names wrong.

ROS starts to protest but he has hardly opened his mouth
before:

CLAUDIUS (*off stage—with urgency*): Ho, Guildenstern!

> GUIL *is still prone. Small pause.*

ROS AND GUIL: You're wanted. . . .

> GUIL *furiously leaps to his feet as* CLAUDIUS *and* GERTRUDE *enter. They are in some desperation.*

CLAUDIUS: Friends both, go join you with some further aid: Hamlet in madness hath Polonius slain, and from his mother's closet hath he dragged him. Go seek him out; speak fair and bring the body into the chapel. I pray you haste in this. (*As he and* GERTRUDE *are hurrying out.*) Come Gertrude, we'll call up our wisest friends and let them know both what we mean to do. . . .

> *They've gone.* ROS *and* GUIL *remain quite still.*

GUIL: Well . . .

ROS: Quite . . .

GUIL: Well, well.

ROS: Quite, quite. (*Nods with spurious confidence.*) Seek him out. (*Pause.*) Etcetera.

GUIL: Quite.

ROS: Well. (*Small pause.*) Well, that's a step in the right direction.

GUIL: You didn't like him?

ROS: Who?

GUIL: Good God, I hope more tears are shed for *us*! . . .

ROS: Well, it's *progress*, isn't it? Something positive. Seek him out. (*Looks round without moving his feet.*) Where does one begin . . . ? (*Takes one step towards the wings and halts.*)

GUIL: Well, that's a step in the right direction.

ROS: You think so? He could be anywhere.

GUIL: All right—you go that way, I'll go this way.

ROS: Right.

> *They walk towards opposite wings.* ROS *halts.*

No.

> GUIL *halts.*

> *You go this way—I'll go that way.*

GUIL: All right.

> *They march towards each other, cross.* ROS *halts.*

ROS: Wait a minute.

> GUIL *halts.*

I think we should stick together. He might be violent.

GUIL: Good point. I'll come with you.

> GUIL *marches across to* ROS. *They turn to leave.* ROS *halts.*

ROS: No, I'll come with *you.*

GUIL: Right.

> *They turn, march across to the opposite wing.* ROS *halts.*

> GUIL *halts.*

ROS: I'll come with *you, my* way.

GUIL: All right.

> *They turn again and march across.* ROS *halts.* GUIL *halts.*

ROS: I've just thought. If we both go, he could come *here.* That would be stupid, wouldn't it?

GUIL: All right—I'll stay, you go.

ROS: Right.

GUIL *marches to midstage.*

I say.

GUIL *wheels and carries on marching back towards* ROS, *who starts marching downstage. They cross.* ROS *halts.*

I've just thought.

GUIL *halts.*

We ought to stick together; he might be violent.

GUIL: Good point.

GUIL *marches down to join* ROS. *They stand still for a moment in their original positions.*

Well, at last we're getting somewhere.

Pause.

Of course, he might not come.

ROS (*airily*): Oh, he'll come.

GUIL: We'd have some explaining to do.

ROS: He'll come. (*Airily wanders upstage.*) Don't worry—take my word for it—(*Looks out—is appalled.*) He's coming!

GUIL: What's he doing?

ROS: Walking.

GUIL: Alone?

ROS: No.

GUIL: Not walking?

ROS: No.

GUIL: Who's with him?

ROS: The old man.

GUIL: Walking?

ROS: No.

GUIL: Ah. That's an opening if ever there was one. (*And is suddenly galvanized into action.*) Let him walk into the trap!

ROS: What trap?

GUIL: You stand there! Don't let him pass!

He positions ROS *with his back to one wing, facing* HAMLET's *entrance.*

GUIL *positions himself next to* ROS, *a few feet away, so that they are covering one side of the stage, facing the opposite side.* GUIL *unfastens his belt.* ROS *does the same. They join the two belts, and hold them taut between them.* ROS's *trousers slide slowly down.*

HAMLET *enters opposite, slowly, dragging* POLONIUS's *body. He enters upstage, makes a small arc and leaves by the same side, a few feet downstage.*

ROS *and* GUIL, *holding the belts taut, stare at him in some bewilderment.*

HAMLET *leaves, dragging the body. They relax the strain on the belts.*

ROS: That was close.

GUIL: There's a limit to what two people can do.

They undo the belts: ROS *pulls up his trousers.*

ROS (*worriedly—he walks a few paces towards* HAMLET's *exit*): He was dead.

GUIL: Of course he's dead!

ROS (*turns to* GUIL): Properly.

GUIL (*angrily*): Death's death, isn't it?

ROS *falls silent. Pause.*

Perhaps he'll come back this way.

ROS *starts to take off his belt.*

No, no, no!—if we can't learn by experience, what else have we got?

ROS *desists.*

Pause.

ROS: Give him a shout.

GUIL: I thought we'd been into all that.

ROS (*shouts*): Hamlet!

GUIL: Don't be absurd.

ROS (*shouts*): Lord Hamlet!

HAMLET *enters.* ROS *is a little dismayed.*

What have you done, my lord, with the dead body?

HAMLET: Compounded it with dust, whereto 'tis kin.

ROS: Tell us where 'tis, that we may take it thence and bear it to the chapel.

HAMLET: Do not believe it.

ROS: Believe what?

HAMLET: That I can keep your counsel and not mine own. Besides, to be demanded of a sponge, what replication should be made by the son of a king?

ROS: Take you me for a sponge, my lord?

HAMLET: Ay, sir, that soaks up the King's countenance, his rewards, his authorities. But such officers do the King best service in the end. He keeps them, like an ape, in the corner of his jaw, first mouthed, to be last swallowed. When he needs what you have gleaned, it is but squeezing you and, sponge, you shall be dry again.

ROS: I understand you not, my lord.

HAMLET: I am glad of it: a knavish speech sleeps in a foolish ear.

ROS: My lord, you must tell us where the body is and go with us to the King.

HAMLET: The body is with the King, but the King is not with the body. The King is a thing——

GUIL: A thing, my lord——?

HAMLET: Of nothing. Bring me to him.

HAMLET *moves resolutely towards one wing. They move with him, shepherding. Just before they reach the exit,* HAMLET, *apparently seeing* CLAUDIUS *approaching from off stage, bends low in a sweeping bow.* ROS *and* GUIL, *cued by Hamlet, also bow deeply—a sweeping ceremonial bow with their cloaks swept round them.* HAMLET, *however, continues the movement into an about-turn and walks off in the opposite direction.* ROS *and* GUIL, *with their heads low, do not notice.*

No one comes on. ROS *and* GUIL *squint upwards and find that they are bowing to nothing.*

CLAUDIUS *enters behind them. At first words they leap up and do a double-take.*

CLAUDIUS: How now? What hath befallen?

ROS: Where the body is bestowed, my lord, we cannot get from him.

CLAUDIUS: But where is he?

ROS (*fractional hesitation*): Without, my lord; guarded to know your pleasure.

CLAUDIUS (*moves*): Bring him before us.

91

This hits ROS *between the eyes but only his eyes show it. Again his hesitation is fractional. And then with great deliberation he turns to* GUIL.

ROS: Ho! Bring in the lord.

Again there is a fractional moment in which ROS *is smug,* GUIL *is trapped and betrayed.* GUIL *opens his mouth and closes it.*

The situation is saved: HAMLET, *escorted, is marched in just as* CLAUDIUS *leaves.* HAMLET *and his* ESCORT *cross the stage and go out, following* CLAUDIUS.

Lighting changes to Exterior.

ROS (*moves to go*): All right, then?

GUIL (*does not move; thoughtfully*): And yet it doesn't seem enough; to have breathed such significance. Can that be all? And why us?—anybody would have done. And we have contributed nothing.

ROS: It was a trying episode while it lasted, but they've done with us now.

GUIL: Done what?

ROS: I don't pretend to have understood. Frankly, I'm not very interested. If they won't tell us, that's their affair. (*He wanders upstage towards the exit.*) For my part, I'm only glad that that's the last we've seen of him—(*And he glances off stage and turns front, his face betraying the fact that* HAMLET *is there.*)

GUIL: I knew it wasn't the end. . . .

ROS (*high*): What else?!

GUIL: We're taking him to England. What's he doing?

ROS *goes upstage and returns.*

ROS: Talking.

GUIL: To himself?

ROS *makes to go,* GUIL *cuts him off.*

Is he alone?

ROS: No, he's with a soldier.

GUIL: Then he's not talking to himself, is he?

ROS: Not *by* himself ... Should we go?

GUIL: Where?

ROS: Anywhere.

GUIL: Why?

ROS *puts up his head listening.*

ROS: There it is again. (*In anguish.*) All I ask is a change of ground!

GUIL (*coda*): Give us this day our daily round. . . .

HAMLET *enters behind them, talking with a soldier in arms.* ROS *and* GUIL *don't look round.*

ROS: They'll have us hanging about till we're dead. At least. And the weather will change. (*Looks up.*) The spring can't last for ever.

HAMLET: Good sir, whose powers are these?

SOLDIER: They are of Norway, sir.

HAMLET: How purposed, sir, I pray you?

SOLDIER: Against some part of Poland.

HAMLET: Who commands them, sir?

SOLDIER: The nephew to old Norway, Fortinbras.

ROS: We'll be cold. The summer won't last.

93

GUIL: It's autumnal.

ROS (*examining the ground*): No leaves.

GUIL: Autumnal—nothing to do with leaves. It is to do with a certain brownness at the edges of the day. . . . Brown is creeping up on us, take my word for it. . . . Russets and tangerine shades of old gold flushing the very outside edge of the senses . . . deep shining ochres, burnt umber and parchments of baked earth—reflecting on itself and through itself, filtering the light. At such times, perhaps, coincidentally, the leaves might fall, somewhere, by repute. Yesterday was blue, like smoke.

ROS (*head up, listening*): I got it again then.

They listen—faintest sound of TRAGEDIANS' *band.*

HAMLET: I humbly thank you, sir.

SOLDIER: God by you, sir. (*Exit.*)

ROS *gets up quickly and goes to* HAMLET.

ROS: Will it please you go, my lord?

HAMLET: I'll be with you straight. Go you a little before.

HAMLET *turns to face upstage.* ROS *returns down.* GUIL *faces front, doesn't turn.*

GUIL: Is he there?

ROS: Yes.

GUIL: What's he doing?

ROS *looks over his shoulder.*

ROS: Talking.

GUIL: To himself?

ROS: Yes.

94

Pause. ROS *makes to leave.*

ROS: He *said* we can go. Cross my heart.

GUIL: I like to know where I am. Even if I don't know where I am, I like to know *that*. If we go there's no knowing.

ROS: No knowing what?

GUIL: If we'll ever come back.

ROS: We don't want to come back.

GUIL: That may very well be true, but do we want to go?

ROS: We'll be free.

GUIL: I don't know. It's the same sky.

ROS: We've come this far.

He moves towards exit. GUIL *follows him.*

And besides, anything could happen yet.

They go.

BLACKOUT

95

ACT THREE

Opens in pitch darkness.
Soft sea sounds.

After several seconds of nothing, a voice from the dark . . .

GUIL: Are you there?

ROS: Where?

GUIL (*bitterly*): A flying start. . . .

    Pause.

ROS: Is that you?

GUIL: Yes.

ROS: How do you know?

GUIL (*explosion*): Oh-for-God's-sake!

ROS: We're not finished, then?

GUIL: Well, we're here, aren't we?

ROS: Are we? I can't see a thing.

GUIL: You can still *think*, can't you?

ROS: I think so.

GUIL: You can still *talk*.

ROS: What should I say?

GUIL: Don't bother. You can *feel*, can't you?

ROS: Ah! There's life in me yet!

GUIL: What are you feeling?

ROS: A leg. Yes, it feels like my leg.

GUIL: How does it feel?

ROS: Dead.

GUIL: Dead?

ROS (*panic*): I can't feel a thing!

GUIL: Give it a pinch! (*Immediately he yelps.*)

ROS: Sorry.

GUIL: Well, that's cleared that up.

*Longer pause: the sound builds a little and identifies itself—
the sea. Ship timbers, wind in the rigging, and then shouts
of sailors calling obscure but inescapably nautical instructions
from all directions, far and near: A short list:*

> Hard a larboard!
> Let go the stays!
> Reef down me hearties!
> Is that you, cox'n?
> Hel-llo! Is that you?
> Hard a port!
> Easy as she goes!
> Keep her steady on the lee!
> Haul away, lads!
> (*Snatches of sea shanty maybe.*)
> Fly the jib!
> Tops'l up, me maties!

When the point has been well made and more so.

ROS: We're on a boat. (*Pause.*) Dark, isn't it?

GUIL: Not for night.

ROS: No, not for *night*.

98

GUIL: Dark for day.

    Pause.

ROS: Oh yes, it's dark for *day.*

GUIL: We must have gone north, of course.

ROS: Off course?

GUIL: Land of the midnight sun, that is.

ROS: Of course.

    Some sailor sounds.

    A lantern is lit upstage—In fact by HAMLET.

    The stage lightens disproportionately—

    Enough to see:

    ROS *and* GUIL *sitting downstage.*

    Vague shapes of rigging, etc., behind.

    I think it's getting light.

GUIL: Not for night.

ROS: This far north.

GUIL: Unless we're off course.

ROS (*small pause*): Of course.
    No, No, No

    A better light—Lantern? Moon? . . . Light.
    Revealing, among other things, three large man-sized casks
    on deck, upended, with lids. Spaced but in line. Behind and
    above—a gaudy striped umbrella, on a pole stuck into the
    deck, tilted so that we do not see behind it—one of those
    huge six-foot-diameter jobs. Still dim upstage. ROS *and* GUIL
    still facing front.

ROS: Yes, it's lighter than it was. It'll be night soon. This far
    north. (*Dolefully.*) I suppose we'll have to go to sleep.
    (*He yawns and stretches.*)

GUIL: Tired?

ROS: No . . . I don't think I'd take to it. Sleep all night, can't see a thing all day. . . . Those eskimos must have a quiet life.

GUIL: Where?

ROS: What?

GUIL: I thought you—— (*Relapses.*) I've lost all capacity for disbelief. I'm not sure that I could even rise to a little gentle scepticism.

   Pause.

ROS: Well, shall we stretch our legs?

GUIL: I don't feel like stretching my legs.

ROS: I'll stretch them for you, if you like.

GUIL: No.

ROS: We could stretch each other's. That way we wouldn't have to go anywhere.

GUIL (*pause*): No, somebody might come in.

ROS: In where?

GUIL: Out here.

ROS: In out here?

GUIL: On deck.

   ROS *considers the floor: slaps it.*

ROS: Nice bit of planking, that.

GUIL: Yes, I'm very fond of boats myself. I like the way they're —contained. You don't have to worry about which way to go, or whether to go at all—the question doesn't arise, because you're on a *boat*, aren't you? Boats are safe areas in the game of tag . . . the players will hold their positions until the music starts. . . . I think I'll spend most of my life on boats. → illusion of freedom

ROS: Very healthy.

ROS inhales with expectation, exhales with boredom. GUIL stands up and looks over the audience.

GUIL: One is free on a boat. For a time. Relatively.

ROS: What's it like?

GUIL: Rough.

ROS joins him. They look out over the audience.

ROS: I think I'm going to be sick.

GUIL licks a finger, holds it up experimentally.

GUIL: Other side, I think.

ROS goes upstage: Ideally a sort of upper deck joined to the downstage lower deck by short steps. The umbrella being on the upper deck. ROS pauses by the umbrella and looks behind it. GUIL meanwhile has been resuming his own theme —looking out over the audience——

Free to move, speak, extemporise, and yet. We have not been cut loose. Our truancy is defined by one fixed star, and our drift represents merely a slight change of angle to it: we may seize the moment, toss it around while the moments pass, a short dash here, an exploration there, but we are brought round full circle to face again the single immutable fact—that we, Rosencrantz and Guildenstern, bearing a letter from one king to another, are taking Hamlet to England.

By which time, ROS has returned, tiptoeing with great import, teeth clenched for secrecy, gets to GUIL, points surreptitiously behind him—and a tight whisper:

ROS: I say—*he's there!*

GUIL (*unsurprised*): What's he doing?

ROS: Sleeping.

GUIL: It's all right for him.

ROS: What is?

GUIL: He can sleep.

ROS: It's all right for him.

GUIL: He's got us now.

ROS: He can sleep.

GUIL: It's all done for him.

ROS: He's got us.

GUIL: And we've got nothing. (*A cry.*) All I ask is our common due!

ROS: For those in peril on the sea. . . .

GUIL: Give us this day our daily cue.

Beat, pause. Sit. Long pause.

ROS (*after shifting, looking around*): What now?

GUIL: What do you mean?

ROS: Well, nothing is happening.

GUIL: We're on a boat.

ROS: I'm aware of that.

GUIL (*angrily*): Then what do you expect? (*Unhappily.*) We act on scraps of information . . . sifting half-remembered directions that we can hardly separate from instinct.

ROS puts a hand into his purse, then both hands behind his back, then holds his fists out.

GUIL taps one fist.

102

ROS *opens it to show a coin.*

He gives it to GUIL.

He puts his hand back into his purse. Then both hands behind his back, then holds his fists out.

GUIL *taps one.*

ROS *opens it to show a coin. He gives it to* GUIL.

Repeat.

Repeat.

GUIL *getting tense. Desperate to lose.*

Repeat.

GUIL *taps a hand, changes his mind, taps the other, and* ROS *inadvertently reveals that he has a coin in both fists.*

GUIL: You had money in both hands.

ROS (*embarrassed*): Yes.

GUIL: Every time?

ROS: Yes.

GUIL: What's the point of that?

ROS (*pathetic*): I wanted to make you happy. (I love you)

    Beat.

GUIL: How much did he give you?

ROS: Who?

GUIL: The King. He gave us some money.

ROS: How much did he give you?

GUIL: I asked you first.

ROS: I got the same as you.

103

GUIL: He wouldn't discriminate between us.

ROS: How much did you get?

GUIL: The same.

ROS: How do you know?

GUIL: You just told me—how do *you* know?

ROS: He wouldn't discriminate between us.

GUIL: Even if he could.

ROS: Which he never could.

GUIL: He couldn't even be sure of mixing us up.

ROS: Without mixing us up.

GUIL (*turning on him furiously*): Why don't you say something original! No wonder the whole thing is so stagnant! You don't take me up on anything—you just repeat it in a different order.

ROS: I can't think of anything original. I'm only good in support.

GUIL: I'm sick of making the running.

ROS (*humbly*): It must be your dominant personality. (*Almost in tears.*) Oh, what's going to become of us! (I love you)

And GUIL comforts him, all harshness gone.

GUIL: Don't cry . . . it's all right . . . there . . . there, I'll see we're all right.

ROS: But we've got nothing to go on, we're out on our own.

GUIL: We're on our way to England—we're taking Hamlet there.

ROS: What for?

GUIL: What for? Where have you been?

ROS: When? (*Pause.*) We won't know what to do when we get there.

104

GUIL: We take him to the King.

ROS: Will *he* be there?

GUIL: No—the king of England.

ROS: He's expecting us?

GUIL: No.

ROS: He won't know what we're playing at. What are we going to *say*?

GUIL: We've got a letter. You remember the letter.

ROS: Do I?

GUIL: Everything is explained in the letter. We count on that.

ROS: Is that it, then?

GUIL: What?

ROS: We take Hamlet to the English king, we hand over the letter—what then?

GUIL: There may be something in the letter to keep us going a bit.

ROS: And if not?

GUIL: Then that's it—we're finished.

ROS: At a loose end?

GUIL: Yes.

Pause.

ROS: Are there likely to be loose ends? (*Pause.*) Who is the English king?

GUIL: That depends on when we get there.

ROS: What do you think it says?

GUIL: Oh . . . greetings. Expressions of loyalty. Asking of favours, calling in of debts. Obscure promises balanced by vague threats. . . . Diplomacy. Regards to the family.

ROS: And about Hamlet?

GUIL: Oh yes.

ROS: And us—the full background?

GUIL: I should say so.

Pause.

ROS: So we've got a letter which explains everything.

GUIL: You've got it.

ROS *takes that literally. He starts to pat his pockets, etc.*

What's the matter?

ROS: The letter.

GUIL: Have you got it?

ROS (*rising fear*): Have I? (*Searches frantically.*) Where would I have put it?

GUIL: You can't have lost it.

ROS: I must have!

GUIL: That's odd—I thought he gave it to me.

ROS *looks at him hopefully.*

ROS: Perhaps he did.

GUIL: But you seemed so sure it was *you* who hadn't got it.

ROS (*high*): It *was* me who hadn't got it!

GUIL: But if he gave it to me there's no reason why you should have had it in the first place, in which case I don't see what all the fuss is about you *not* having it.

ROS (*pause*): I admit it's confusing.

GUIL: This is all getting rather undisciplined. . . . The boat, the night, the sense of isolation and uncertainty . . . all these induce a loosening of the concentration. We must not lose control. Tighten up. Now. Either you have lost the letter or you didn't have it to lose in the first place, in which case the King never gave it to you, in which case he gave it to me, in which case I would have put it into my inside top pocket, in which case (*calmly producing the letter*) . . . it will be . . . here. (*They smile at each other.*) We mustn't drop off like that again.

Pause. ROS *takes the letter gently from him.*

ROS: Now that we have found it, why were we looking for it?

GUIL (*thinks*): We thought it was lost.

ROS: Something else?

GUIL: No.

Deflation.

ROS: Now we've lost the tension.

GUIL: What tension?

ROS: What was the last thing I said before we wandered off?

GUIL: When was that?

ROS (*helplessly*): I can't remember.

GUIL (*leaping up*): What a shambles! We're just not getting anywhere.

ROS (*mournfully*): Not even England. I don't believe in it anyway.

GUIL: What?

ROS: England.

GUIL: Just a conspiracy of cartographers, you mean?

ROS: I mean I don't believe it! (*Calmer.*) I have no image. I try

to picture us arriving, a little harbour perhaps . . . roads
. . . inhabitants to point the way . . . horses on the road . . .
riding for a day or a fortnight and then a palace and the
English king. . . . That would be the logical kind of thing.
. . . But my mind remains a blank. No. We're slipping off
the map.

GUIL: Yes . . . yes. . . . (*Rallying.*) But you don't believe anything
till it happens. And it *has* all happened. Hasn't it?

ROS: We drift down time, clutching at straws. But what good's
a brick to a drowning man?

GUIL: Don't give up, we can't be long now.

ROS: We might as well be dead. Do you think death could possibly
be a boat?

GUIL: No, no, no . . . Death is . . . not. Death isn't. You take
my meaning. Death is the ultimate negative. Not-being.
You can't not-be on a boat.

ROS: I've frequently not been on boats.

GUIL: No, no, no—what you've been is not on boats.

ROS: I wish I was dead. (*Considers the drop.*) I could jump over
the side. That would put a spoke in their wheel.

GUIL: Unless they're counting on it.

ROS: I shall remain on board. That'll put a spoke in their wheel.
(*The futility of it, fury.*) All right! We don't question, we
don't doubt. We perform. But a line must be drawn
somewhere, and I would like to put it on record that I have
no confidence in England. Thank you. (*Thinks about this.*)
And even if it's true, it'll just be another shambles.

GUIL: I don't see why.

ROS (*furious*): He won't know what we're talking about.—What
are we going to *say*?

108

GUIL: We say—Your majesty, we have arrived!

ROS (*kingly*): And who are you?

GUIL: We are Rosencrantz and Guildenstern.

ROS (*barks*): Never heard of you!

GUIL: Well, we're nobody special——

ROS (*regal and nasty*): What's your game?

GUIL: We've got our instructions——

ROS: First I've heard of it——

GUIL (*angry*): Let me finish—— (*Humble.*) We've come from Denmark.

ROS: What do you want?

GUIL: Nothing—we're delivering Hamlet——

ROS: Who's he?

GUIL (*irritated*): You've heard of *him*——

ROS: Oh, I've heard of him all right and I want nothing to do with it.

GUIL: But——

ROS: You march in here without so much as a by-your-leave and expect me to take in every lunatic you try to pass off with a lot of unsubstantiated——

GUIL: We've got a letter——

ROS *snatches it and tears it open.*

ROS (*efficiently*): I see . . . I see . . . well, this seems to support your story such as it is—it is an exact command from the king of Denmark, for several different reasons, importing Denmark's health and England's too, that on the reading of this letter, without delay, I should have Hamlet's head cut off——!

GUIL *snatches the letter.* ROS, *double-taking, snatches it back.*
GUIL *snatches it half back. They read it together, and separate.*

Pause.

They are well downstage looking front.

ROS: The sun's going down. It will be dark soon.

GUIL: Do you think so?

ROS: I was just making conversation. (*Pause.*) We're his *friends.*

GUIL: How do you know?

ROS: From our young days brought up with him.

GUIL: You've only got their word for it.

ROS: But that's what we depend on.

GUIL: Well, yes, and then again no. (*Airily.*) Let us keep things
in proportion. Assume, if you like, that they're going to
kill him. Well, he is a man, he is mortal, death comes to us
all, etcetera, and consequently he would have died anyway,
sooner or later. Or to look at it from the social point of
view—he's just one man among many, the loss would be
well within reason and convenience. And then again, what
is so terrible about death? As Socrates so philosophically
put it, since we don't know what death is, it is illogical to
fear it. It might be . . . very nice. Certainly it is a release
from the burden of life, and, for the godly, a haven and a
reward. Or to look at it another way—we are little men, we
don't know the ins and outs of the matter, there are wheels
within wheels, etcetera—it would be presumptuous of us to
interfere with the designs of fate or even of kings. All in all, I
think we'd be well advised to leave well alone. Tie up the
letter—there—neatly—like that.—They won't notice the
broken seal, assuming you were in character.

ROS: But what's the point?

GUIL: Don't apply logic.

ROS: He's done nothing to us.

GUIL: Or justice.

ROS: It's awful.

GUIL: But it could have been worse. I was beginning to think it was. (*And his relief comes out in a laugh.*)

Behind them HAMLET *appears from behind the umbrella. The light has been going. Slightly.* HAMLET *is going to the lantern.*

ROS: The position as I see it, then. We, Rosencrantz and Guildenstern, from our young days brought up with him, awakened by a man standing on his saddle, are summoned, and arrive, and are instructed to glean what afflicts him and draw him on to pleasures, such as a play, which unfortunately, as it turns out, is abandoned in some confusion owing to certain nuances outside our appreciation —which, among other causes, results in, among other effects, a high, not to say, homicidal, excitement in Hamlet, whom we, in consequence, are escorting, for his own good, to England. Good. We're on top of it now.

HAMLET blows out the lantern. The stage goes pitch black. The black resolves itself to moonlight, by which HAMLET *approaches the sleeping* ROS *and* GUIL. *He extracts the letter and takes it behind his umbrella; the light of his lantern shines through the fabric,* HAMLET *emerges again with a letter, and replaces it, and retires, blowing out his lantern.*

Morning comes.

ROS *watches it coming—from the auditorium. Behind him is a gay sight. Beneath the re-tilted umbrella, reclining in a deck-chair, wrapped in a rug, reading a book, possibly smoking, sits* HAMLET.

111

ROS *watches the morning come, and brighten to high noon.*

ROS: I'm assuming nothing. (*He stands up.* GUIL *wakes.*)
The position as I see it, then. That's west unless we're off
course, in which case it's night; the King gave me the same as
you, the King gave you the same as me; the King never gave
me the letter, the King gave you the letter, we don't know
what's in the letter; we take Hamlet to the English king, it
depending on when we get there who he is, and we hand
over the letter, which may or may not have something in it
to keep us going, and if not, we are finished and at a loose
end, if they have loose ends. We could have done worse. I
don't think we missed any chances. . . . Not that we're
getting much help. (*He sits down again. They lie down—
prone.*) If we stopped breathing we'd vanish.

*The muffled sound of a recorder. They sit up with
disproportionate interest.*

GUIL: Here we go.

ROS: Yes, but what?

They listen to the music.

GUIL (*excitedly*): Out of the void, finally, a sound; while on a
boat (admittedly) outside the action (admittedly) the perfect
and absolute silence of the wet lazy slap of water against
water and the rolling creak of timber—breaks; giving rise
at once to the speculation or the assumption or the hope
that something is about to happen; a pipe is heard. One of
the sailors has pursed his lips against a woodwind, his fingers
and thumb governing, shall we say, the ventages, whereupon,
giving it breath, let us say, with his mouth, it, the pipe,
discourses, as the saying goes, most eloquent music. A
thing like that, it could change the course of events.
(*Pause.*) Go and see what it is.

ROS: It's someone playing on a pipe.

GUIL: Go and find him.

ROS: And then what?

GUIL: I don't know—request a tune.

ROS: What for?

GUIL: Quick—before we lose our momentum.

ROS: Why!—something is happening. It had quite escaped my attention!

He listens: Makes a stab at an exit. Listens more carefully: Changes direction.

GUIL *takes no notice.*

ROS *wanders about trying to decide where the music comes from. Finally he tracks it down—unwillingly—to the middle barrel. There is no getting away from it. He turns to* GUIL *who takes no notice.* ROS, *during this whole business, never quite breaks into articulate speech. His face and his hands indicate his incredulity. He stands gazing at the middle barrel. The pipe plays on within. He kicks the barrel. The pipe stops. He leaps back towards* GUIL. *The pipe starts up again. He approaches the barrel cautiously. He lifts the lid. The music is louder. He slams down the lid. The music is softer. He goes back towards* GUIL. *But a drum starts, muffled. He freezes. He turns. Considers the left-hand barrel. The drumming goes on within, in time to the flute. He walks back to* GUIL. *He opens his mouth to speak. Doesn't make it. A lute is heard. He spins round at the third barrel. More instruments join in. Until it is quite inescapable that inside the three barrels, distributed, playing together a familiar tune which has been heard three times before, are the* TRAGEDIANS.

They play on.

ROS *sits beside* GUIL. *They stare ahead.*

The tune comes to an end.

113

Pause.

ROS: I thought I heard a band. (*In anguish.*) Plausibility is all I presume!

GUIL (*coda*): Call us this day our daily tune. . . .

The lid of the middle barrel flies open and the PLAYER's *head pops out.*

PLAYER: Aha! All in the same boat, then! (*He climbs out. He goes round banging on the barrels.*)

Everybody out!

Impossibly, the TRAGEDIANS *climb out of the barrels. With their instruments, but not their cart. A few bundles. Except* ALFRED. *The* PLAYER *is cheerful.*

(*To* ROS:) Where are we?

ROS: Travelling.

PLAYER: Of course, we haven't got there yet.

ROS: Are we all right for England?

PLAYER: You look all right to me. I don't think they're very particular in England. Al-l-fred!

ALFRED *emerges from the* PLAYER's *barrel.*

GUIL: What are you doing here?

PLAYER: Travelling. (*To* TRAGEDIANS:) Right—blend into the background!

The TRAGEDIANS *are in costume (from the mime): A King with crown,* ALFRED *as Queen, Poisoner and the two cloaked figures.*

They blend.

(*To* GUIL:) Pleased to see us? (*Pause.*) You've come out of it very well, so far.

GUIL: And you?

PLAYER: In disfavour. Our play offended the King.

GUIL: Yes.

PLAYER: Well, he's a second husband himself. Tactless, really.

ROS: It was quite a good play nevertheless.

PLAYER: We never really got going—it was getting quite interesting when they stopped it.

Looks up at HAMLET.

That's the way to travel. . . .

GUIL: What were you doing in there?

PLAYER: Hiding. (*Indicating costumes.*) We had to run for it just as we were.

ROS: Stowaways.

PLAYER: Naturally—we didn't get paid, owing to circumstances ever so slightly beyond our control, and all the money we had we lost betting on certainties. Life is a gamble, at terrible odds—if it was a bet you wouldn't take it. Did you know that any number doubled is even?

ROS: Is it?

PLAYER: We learn something every day, to our cost. But we troupers just go on and on. Do you know what happens to old actors?

ROS: What?

PLAYER: Nothing. They're still acting. Surprised, then?

GUIL: What?

PLAYER: Surprised to see us?

GUIL: I knew it wasn't the end.

PLAYER: With practically everyone on his feet. What do you make of it, so far?

GUIL: We haven't got much to go on.

PLAYER: You speak to him?

ROS: It's possible.

GUIL: But it wouldn't make any difference.

ROS: But it's possible.

GUIL: Pointless.

ROS: It's allowed.

GUIL: Allowed, yes. We are not restricted. No boundaries have been defined, no inhibitions imposed. We have, for the while, secured, or blundered into, our release, for the while. Spontaneity and whim are the order of the day. Other wheels are turning but they are not our concern. We can breathe. We can relax. We can do what we like and say what we like to whomever we like, without restriction.

ROS: Within limits, of course.

GUIL: Certainly within limits.

> HAMLET *comes down to footlights and regards the audience. The others watch but don't speak.* HAMLET *clears his throat noisily and spits into the audience. A split second later he claps his hand to his eye and wipes himself. He goes back upstage.*

ROS: A compulsion towards philosophical introspection is his chief characteristic, if I may put it like that. It does not mean he is mad. It does not mean he isn't. Very often, it does not mean anything at all. Which may or may not be a kind of madness.

GUIL: It really boils down to symptoms. Pregnant replies, mystic allusions, mistaken identities, arguing his father is

116

his mother, that sort of thing; intimations of suicide, forgoing of exercise, loss of mirth, hints of claustrophobia not to say delusions of imprisonment; invocations of camels, chameleons, capons, whales, weasels, hawks, handsaws—riddles, quibbles and evasions; amnesia, paranoia, myopia; day-dreaming, hallucinations; stabbing his elders, abusing his parents, insulting his lover, and appearing hatless in public—knock-kneed, droop-stockinged and sighing like a love-sick schoolboy, which at his age is coming on a bit strong.

ROS: And talking to himself.

GUIL: And talking to himself.

ROS *and* GUIL *move apart together.*

Well, where has that got us?

ROS: He's the Player.

GUIL: His play offended the King——

ROS: —offended the King——

GUIL: —who orders his arrest——

ROS: —orders his arrest——

GUIL: —so he escapes to England——

ROS: On the boat to which he meets——

GUIL: Guildenstern and Rosencrantz taking Hamlet——

ROS: —who also offended the King——

GUIL: —and killed Polonius——

ROS: —offended the King in a variety of ways——

GUIL: —to England. (*Pause.*) That seems to be it.

ROS *jumps up.*

ROS: Incidents! All we get is incidents! Dear God, is it too much to expect a little sustained action?!

And on the word, the PIRATES attack. That is to say: Noise and shouts and rushing about. "Pirates."

Everyone visible goes frantic. HAMLET draws his sword and rushes downstage. GUIL, ROS and PLAYER draw swords and rush upstage. Collision. HAMLET turns back up. They turn back down. Collision. By which time there is general panic right upstage. All four charge upstage with ROS, GUIL and PLAYER shouting:

> At last!
> To arms!
> Pirates!
> Up there!
> Down there!
> To my sword's length!
> Action!

All four reach the top, see something they don't like, waver, run for their lives downstage:

HAMLET, in the lead, leaps into the left barrel. PLAYER leaps into the right barrel. ROS and GUIL leap into the middle barrel. All closing the lids after them.

The lights dim to nothing while the sound of fighting continues. The sound fades to nothing. The lights come up. The middle barrel (ROS's and GUIL's) is missing.

The lid of the right-hand barrel is raised cautiously, the heads of ROS and GUIL appear.

The lid of the other barrel (HAMLET's) is raised. The head of the PLAYER appears.

All catch sight of each other and slam down lids.

Pause.

Lids raised cautiously.

ROS (*relief*): They've gone. (*He starts to climb out.*) That was close. I've never thought quicker.

They are all three out of barrels. GUIL *is wary and nervous.* ROS *is light-headed. The* PLAYER *is phlegmatic. They note the missing barrel.*

ROS *looks round.*

ROS: Where's——?

The PLAYER *takes off his hat in mourning.*

PLAYER: Once more, alone—on our own resources.

GUIL (*worried*): What do you mean? Where is he?

PLAYER: Gone.

GUIL: Gone where?

PLAYER: Yes, we were dead lucky there. If that's the word I'm after.

ROS (*not a pick up*): Dead?

PLAYER: Lucky.

ROS (*he means*): Is he dead?

PLAYER: Who knows?

GUIL (*rattled*): He's not coming back?

PLAYER: Hardly.

ROS: He's dead then. He's dead as far as we're concerned.

PLAYER: Or we are as far as he is. (*He goes and sits on the floor to one side.*) Not too bad, is it?

GUIL (*rattled*): But he can't—we're supposed to be—we've got a *letter*—we're going to England with a letter for the King——

119

PLAYER: Yes, that much seems certain. I congratulate you on the unambiguity of your situation.

GUIL: But you don't understand—it contains—we've had our instructions——the whole thing's pointless without him.

PLAYER: Pirates could happen to anyone. Just deliver the letter. They'll send ambassadors from England to explain. . . .

GUIL (*worked up*): Can't you see—the pirates left us home and high—dry and home—drome——(*Furiously*.) The pirates left us high and dry!

PLAYER (*comforting*): There . . .

GUIL (*near tears*): Nothing will be resolved without him. . . .

PLAYER: There . . . !

GUIL: We need Hamlet for our release!

PLAYER: There!

GUIL: What are we supposed to do?

PLAYER: This.

He turns away, lies down if he likes. ROS *and* GUIL *apart*.

ROS: Saved again.

GUIL: Saved for what?

ROS *sighs*.

ROS: The sun's going down. (*Pause*.) It'll be night soon. (*Pause*.) If that's west. (*Pause*.) Unless we've——

GUIL (*shouts*): Shut up! I'm sick of it! Do you think conversation is going to help us now?

ROS (*hurt, desperately ingratiating*): I—I bet you all the money I've got the year of my birth doubled is an odd number.

GUIL (*moan*): No-o.

120

ROS: *Your* birth!

GUIL *smashes him down.*

GUIL (*broken*): We've travelled too far, and our momentum has taken over; we move idly towards eternity, without possibility of reprieve or hope of explanation.

ROS: Be happy—if you're not even *happy* what's so good about surviving? (*He picks himself up.*) We'll be all right. I suppose we just go on.

GUIL: Go where?

ROS: To England.

GUIL: England! *That's* a dead end. I never believed in it anyway.

ROS: All we've got to do is make our report and that'll be that. Surely.

GUIL: I don't *believe* it—a shore, a harbour, say—and we get off and we stop someone and say—Where's the King?— And he says, Oh, you follow that road there and take the first left and—— (*Furiously.*) I don't believe any of it!

ROS: It doesn't sound very plausible.

GUIL: And even if we came face to face, what do we say?

ROS: We say—We've arrived!

GUIL (*kingly*): And who are you?

ROS: We are Guildenstern and Rosencrantz.

GUIL: Which is which?

ROS: Well, I'm—You're—— who's who?

GUIL: What's it all about?——

ROS: Well, we were bringing Hamlet—but then some pirates——

GUIL: I don't begin to understand. Who are all these people, what's it got to do with me? You turn up out of the blue with some cock and bull story——

ROS (*with letter*): We have a letter——

GUIL (*snatches it, opens it*): A letter—yes—that's true. That's something . . . a letter . . . (*Reads.*) "As England is Denmark's faithful tributary . . . as love between them like the palm might flourish, etcetera . . . that on the knowing of this contents, without delay of any kind, should those bearers, Rosencrantz and Guildenstern, put to sudden death——"

He double-takes. ROS *snatches the letter.* GUIL *snatches it back.* ROS *snatches it half back. They read it again and look up.*

The PLAYER *gets to his feet and walks over to his barrel and kicks it and shouts into it.*

PLAYER: They've gone! It's all over!

One by one the PLAYERS *emerge, impossibly, from the barrel, and form a casually menacing circle round* ROS *and* GUIL, *who are still appalled and mesmerised.*

GUIL (*quietly*): Where we went wrong was getting on a boat. We can move, of course, change direction, rattle about, but our movement is contained within a larger one that carries us along as inexorably as the wind and current. . . .

ROS: They had it in for us, didn't they? Right from the beginning. Who'd have thought that we were so important?

GUIL: But why? Was it all for this? Who are we that so much should converge on our little deaths? (*In anguish to the* PLAYER:) Who are *we*?

PLAYER: You are Rosencrantz and Guildenstern. That's enough.

GUIL: No—it is not enough. To be told so little—to such an end— and still, finally, to be denied an explanation——

PLAYER: In our experience, most things end in death.

GUIL (*fear, vengeance, scorn*): Your experience!—*Actors!*

He snatches a dagger from the PLAYER's *belt and holds the point at the* PLAYER's *throat: the* PLAYER *backs and* GUIL *advances, speaking more quietly.*

I'm talking about death—and you've never experienced *that.* And you cannot *act* it. You die a thousand casual deaths—with none of that intensity which squeezes out life . . . and no blood runs cold anywhere. Because even as you die you know that you will come back in a different hat. But no one gets up after *death*—there is no applause—there is only silence and some second-hand clothes, and that's—*death*——

And he pushes the blade in up to the hilt. The PLAYER *stands with huge, terrible eyes, clutches at the wound as the blade withdraws: he makes small weeping sounds and falls to his knees, and then right down.*

While he is dying, GUIL, *nervous, high, almost hysterical, wheels on the* TRAGEDIANS——

If we have a destiny, then so had he—and if this is ours, then that was his—and if there are no explanations for us, then let there be none for him——

The TRAGEDIANS *watch the* PLAYER *die: they watch with some interest. The* PLAYER *finally lies still. A short moment of silence. Then the* TRAGEDIANS *start to applaud with genuine admiration. The* PLAYER *stands up, brushing himself down.*

PLAYER (*modestly*): Oh, come, come, gentlemen—no flattery—it was merely competent——

The TRAGEDIANS *are still congratulating him. The* PLAYER *approaches* GUIL, *who stands rooted, holding the dagger.*

PLAYER: What did you think? (*Pause.*) You see, it *is* the kind they do believe in—it's what is expected.

He holds his hand out for the dagger. GUIL *slowly puts the point of the dagger on to the* PLAYER's *hand, and pushes . . . the blade slides back into the handle. The* PLAYER *smiles, reclaims the dagger.*

For a moment you thought I'd—cheated.

ROS *relieves his own tension with loud nervy laughter.*

ROS: Oh, very good! *Very* good! Took me in completely—didn't he take you in completely—(*claps his hands*). Encore! Encore!

PLAYER (*activated, arms spread, the professional*): Deaths for all ages and occasions! Deaths by suspension, convulsion, consumption, incision, execution, asphyxiation and malnutrition—! Climactic carnage, by poison and by steel—! Double deaths by duel—! Show!—

ALFRED, *still in his Queen's costume, dies by poison: the* PLAYER, *with rapier, kills the* "KING" *and duels with a fourth* TRAGEDIAN, *inflicting and receiving a wound. The two remaining* TRAGEDIANS, *the two* "SPIES" *dressed in the same coats as* ROS *and* GUIL, *are stabbed, as before. And the light is fading over the deaths which take place right upstage.*

(*Dying amid the dying—tragically; romantically.*) So there's an end to that—it's commonplace: light goes with life, and in the winter of your years the dark comes early. . . .

GUIL (*tired, drained, but still an edge of impatience; over the mime*): No . . . no . . . not for *us*, not like that. Dying is not romantic, and death is not a game which will soon be over . . . Death is not anything . . . death is not . . . It's the absence of presence, nothing more . . . the endless time of never coming back . . . a gap you can't see, and when the wind blows through it, it makes no sound. . . .

The light has gone upstage. Only GUIL *and* ROS *are visible as* ROS's *clapping falters to silence.*

Small pause.

ROS: That's it, then, is it?

No answer. He looks out front.

The sun's going down. Or the earth's coming up, as the fashionable theory has it.

Small pause.

Not that it makes any difference.

Pause.

What was it all about? When did it begin?

Pause. No answer.

Couldn't we just stay put? I mean no one is going to come on and drag us off. . . . They'll just have to wait. We're still young . . . fit . . . we've got years. . . .

Pause. No answer.

(*A cry.*) We've done nothing wrong! We didn't harm anyone. Did we?

GUIL: I can't remember.

ROS *pulls himself together.*

ROS: All right, then. I don't care. I've had enough. To tell you the truth, I'm relieved.

And he disappears from view. GUIL *does not notice.*

GUIL: Our names shouted in a certain dawn . . . a message . . . a summons . . . There must have been a moment, at the beginning, where we could have said—no. But somehow we missed it. (*He looks round and sees he is alone.*)

Rosen—?
Guil—?

He gathers himself.

Well, we'll know better next time. Now you see me, now you— (*and disappears*).

Immediately the whole stage is lit up, revealing, upstage, arranged in the approximate positions last held by the dead TRAGEDIANS, *the tableau of court and corpses which is the last scene of* Hamlet.

That is: The KING, QUEEN, LAERTES *and* HAMLET *all dead.* HORATIO *holds* HAMLET. FORTINBRAS *is there.*

So are two AMBASSADORS *from England.*

AMBASSADOR: The sight is dismal;
    and our affairs from England come too late.
    The ears are senseless that should give us hearing
    to tell him his commandment is fulfilled,
    that Rosencrantz and Guildenstern are dead.
    Where should we have our thanks?

HORATIO: Not from his mouth,
    had it the ability of life to thank you:
    He never gave commandment for their death.
    But since, so jump upon this bloody question,
    you from the Polack wars, and you from England,
    are here arrived, give order that these bodies
    high on a stage be placed to the view;
    and let me speak to the yet unknowing world
    how these things came about: so shall you hear
    of carnal, bloody and unnatural acts,
    of accidental judgments, casual slaughters,
    of deaths put on by cunning and forced cause,
    and, in this upshot, purposes mistook
    fallen on the inventors' heads: all this can I
    truly deliver.

But during the above speech, the play fades out, overtaken by dark and music.